Foundations for Living
(2 Timothy, Titus, Philemon)

Foundations for Living
(2 Timothy, Titus, Philemon)

David M. Gower

This book has been prepared primarily for group study in connection with the Adult Teacher's Guide, available for $2.25 from Regular Baptist Press. A transparency packet with sixteen sheets is available. This book may be used for individual instruction. A large-print edition is also available.

REGULAR BAPTIST PRESS
1300 North Meacham Road
Post Office Box 95500
Schaumburg, Illinois 60195

About the Author

David M. Gower is Associate Professor of Bible, Los Angeles Baptist College, Newhall, California. Prior to assuming this faculty position, Mr. Gower served as pastor of Trinity Baptist Church, Pasadena, California, for nine years.

Mr. Gower earned the Th.B. degree from Baptist Bible College of Pennsylvania, the M.Div. from Northwest Baptist Seminary and the Th.M. from Talbot Theological Seminary.

Mr. Gower wrote a series of articles for the Regular Baptist Press adult take-home paper which has subsequently been printed in book form, *Questions of the Charismatics.* He is the author of the current Bible study series in the *Baptist Bulletin.* This is his first series of adult Sunday School materials for Regular Baptist Press.

Mr. Gower and his wife have two children. The family resides in Altadena, California.

FOUNDATIONS FOR LIVING
Adult Student Manual
Vol. 32, No. 3
© 1984 by Regular Baptist Press, Schaumburg, Illinois
Merle R. Hull, Executive Editor
Printed in U.S.A.

Contents

Preface

Panning for gold has led some prospectors to fabulous discoveries and others to despair. Everything depends on the richness of the ore. Be prepared to find great treasures this quarter as you dig into the "mother lode" of Philemon, Titus and 2 Timothy.

These three books focus upon *forgiveness, righteousness* and *faithfulness,* three foundation stones for living. We enter upon the Christian life as God grants us forgiveness in Jesus Christ. As we grow in Christ our lives become increasingly characterized by righteousness. And God expects faithfulness from us, His servants, until He takes us home to be with Him.

You will need your spiritual tools to mine the nuggets. We suggest you begin each chapter of this book with the psalmist's prayer, "Open thou mine eyes, that I may behold wondrous things out of thy law."

The daily Bible readings provide background or commentary for the lessons. They average about ten verses in length and will greatly enhance your study. Why not determine right now to read them each day. If you memorize the suggested memory verses, the Holy Spirit can bring them to your mind just when you need them most. Some of the "Search and Ponder" questions can be answered from the daily Bible readings. Some of them are answered within the pages of this book. Some of them require you to ponder a moment before you give a personal answer.

Read each epistle completely through at least once before studying it. This really helps you to put the pieces together.

I trust God's Spirit will challenge you to greater understanding and more diligent living through Philemon, Titus and 2 Timothy.

1 A Slave's Second Chance

**Verse
to
Memorize**

Philemon 17, 18—"If thou count me therefore a partner, receive him as myself. If he hath wronged thee, or oweth thee ought, put that on mine account."

**Daily
Bible
Readings**

Monday—Paul Goes to Jerusalem—Acts 21:15-26

Tuesday—Trouble in the Temple—Acts 21:27-40

Wednesday—Conspiracy to Murder—Acts 23:11-22

Thursday—Smuggled to Safety—Acts 23:23-35

Friday—Languishing in Jail—Acts 24:1, 24-27; 25:1, 10-12

Saturday—An Accident en Route—Acts 27:27-44

Sunday—Paul Arrives in Rome—Acts 28:11-31

**Search
and
Ponder**

1. Where was Paul as he wrote to Philemon (Philemon 1, 9, 10)? _____

2. Where did Philemon's church meet (vv. 1, 2)? _____

3. When Paul prayed for Philemon, what did he request (v. 6)? _____

_____

4. How old was Paul when he wrote this letter (v. 9)? _____

5. What was the relationship between Philemon and Onesimus (v. 16)? _____

6. What was Philemon to do with Onesimus' unpaid bills (v. 18)? _____

7. What would refresh or bless Paul's heart (v. 20)? _____

8. How could you and your church show love toward all the saints? _____

_____

9. Several times God allowed the outstanding apostle Paul to languish in a prison. Did Paul suffer that way because he lacked faith at those times? (See Hebrews 11:35-38.) _____

10. A false assumption contributed to a riot in the temple (Acts 21:29, 30) and to Paul's arrest (Acts 21:33, 37, 38). No one knows how many times false suppositions have created problems in local churches. What can a person do to prevent this? ___

_____

_____

_____

**Bible
Portion
to Read**   Philemon 1-25

The "Colossian Evening News" featured an unbelievable but true story! "Onesimus, a runaway slave belonging to Philemon, returned to his master. Neighbors said they were shocked to see the missing slave simply walk up to Philemon's house and enter the door.

"Owner Philemon declined to make a statement to the press until tomorrow, but he did give reporters assurances that he would not seek any retaliation against the returned slave.

"Police records show the slave was reported missing nearly a year ago. It was speculated at that time that he had taken a sizable amount of cash when he fled. No one knows where he has been, but most assume he fled to a large city, perhaps Ephesus, Corinth or Athens. Some say he could have gone as far as Rome.

"The warm reception granted to the slave by Philemon and his family has stirred curiosity. We will have more details as they become available."

The United States abolished slavery a century ago, and so most of us have no firsthand experience with slaves or slavery. However, the Roman Empire, into which the Church was born, moved on the backs of slaves. Estimates run as high as six or seven million slaves in the empire during the days of the apostle Paul.

Many of these slaves served as teachers or in other "respectable" positions, though some did hard labor forcibly. But no matter what type of service they rendered, the slaves had no protection under the law and no legal rights. They were considered as mere living property or live instruments. Through the smallest offense to their masters they could be scourged, mutilated, crucified or thrown to the wild beasts. A slave who ran away faced almost certain death should he ever be caught.

A Runaway Is Saved

Onesimus, slave of Philemon, a Christian living in Colosse, ran away from his master. He made his way to Rome and somehow came into contact with the imprisoned apostle Paul. Paul preached the gospel to Onesimus, and Onesimus gloriously trusted Christ. He began to serve Paul and to grow in the grace and knowledge of his Lord and Savior, Jesus Christ.

Onesimus' past came to Paul's attention, and Paul faced the searching problem of what to do with the runaway slave now converted to Christ. Paul knew Onesimus must return to his master, and in the providence of Almighty God, that master was also a believer in Christ and known to Paul! Paul conscientiously and graciously composed a message to the master, Philemon. He explained that Onesimus was a new creature in Christ and urged Philemon to receive him back just as though he were receiving Paul himself.

Paul sent Onesimus on his way back to Philemon but not alone. In his hand Onesimus held the precious letter from Paul which we are now studying. At his side was Tychicus, a Christian brother who shared his journey, his struggles and his dramatic arrival at Colosse (Col. 4:7-9). The words Paul wrote now seize our attention. But first, why was Paul writing from jail?

How Paul Got into Jail

The apostle Paul had concluded his third missionary journey and made a trip to Jerusalem to visit the saints there and to take them gifts from the Gentile Christians. In Jerusalem he was recognized by those who bitterly opposed his message of faith in Christ. These opposition leaders stirred up a riot against Paul as he came into the temple. Roman soldiers intervened, taking Paul into custody and actually saving his life. You find the story in Acts 21.

Paul sat in prison for over two years while the Roman authorities of Palestine wavered about what to do with him. The Jewish leaders kept pressing the Romans to have Paul executed.

Finally, Paul felt there was no way out except to assert his Roman citizenship and ask to go to Caesar for a hearing. He said, "I stand at Caesar's judgment seat, where I ought to be judged. . . . I appeal unto Caesar" (Acts 25:10, 11).

After a long, arduous trip, Paul the prisoner finally arrived at Rome. His traveling companion, Dr. Luke, reported, "And when we came to Rome, the centurion delivered the prisoners to the captain of the guard: but Paul was [permitted] to dwell by himself with a soldier that kept him" (Acts 28:16). Luke continued, "And Paul dwelt two whole years in his own hired house, and received all that came in unto him, preaching the kingdom of God, and teaching those things which concern the Lord Jesus Christ, with all confidence, no man forbidding him" (Acts 28:30, 31).

From that imprisonment or house arrest in Rome Paul wrote several letters by the inspiration of the Holy Spirit. This letter to Philemon is one of them, and so Paul began it by calling himself a prisoner of Jesus Christ.

> This Christian man [Philemon] had a heart of caring concern for the saints in Colosse. His heart of concern showed itself in loving actions, helping those who named Christ as Savior.

Paul's Letter

Paul addressed this letter to Philemon, a Christian man who lived in the city of Colosse, to Apphia, who was probably Philemon's wife, and to Archippus, probably the son of Philemon and Apphia. The church which met in their house was also included in the introduction (v. 2).

Paul's Prayers for Philemon

Prayers of thanks. Paul was very thankful for his Christian brother Philemon and for all the good things he had been hearing about Philemon (vv. 4, 5). Reports of Philemon's growth in love and faith had reached Rome. This Christian man had a heart of caring concern for the saints in Colosse. His heart of concern showed itself in loving actions, helping those who named Christ as Savior.

Philemon trusted Christ and was confident that Christ's teaching should be obeyed. Therefore, his life of good works showed to others that he was relying on the faithful God. The display of Philemon's love and his faith gave him a reputation which traveled all the way to Rome. For that Paul was very thankful.

Often we associate certain characteristics with people. Perhaps we think of physical characteristics like height, hair color or a style of clothing. Perhaps we associate some personality trait, like a short temper, with someone. In Philemon's case Paul thought of love toward the brothers and faith toward God. What are the spiritual characteristics that people associate with you and me when they think about us?

Prayers for Philemon. When Paul prayed for Philemon, he asked God to do a work in this great man. This is found in verse 6, the most difficult verse in the book. Let's start at the end of the verse. God had been developing some good things in Philemon, especially faith and love, as he grew in the Christian walk.

These character qualities were a result of his steadfastness in the Christian faith. That faith had moved him to "communicate" with others. "Communication" here probably means sharing his material possessions by giving money to others.

Paul was concerned that those who saw him being generous would not think that his generosity was mere human kindness. Rather, Paul wanted them to realize that Philemon's generosity was a display of Christian character.

So he prayed that everybody might recognize that Philemon's communication came from the good things within him, created there by Jesus Christ. And Paul prayed that those who observed Philemon might then give glory to the Lord.

Paul also anticipated that a man of such character would rise above the flesh and customs of his day to forgive his runaway slave.

Paul's appeal for Onesimus. Paul wrote to ask that Philemon forgive Onesimus. Paul could have just ordered him to do that and have been confident that Philemon would do as God's

15

apostle instructed. But Paul did not follow that course. Instead, he made an appeal to Philemon, asking him to forgive on the basis of his love for Paul and for other Christians (vv. 8-10).

Paul reinforced his appeal by reminding Philemon that he, Paul, was old and in prison. Certainly the mention of Paul's imprisonment would remind Philemon of how faithful Paul had been to God's teachings, even in extreme difficulties, and it would motivate Philemon to be faithful in doing the right thing with Onesimus.

The name "Onesimus" meant "profitable." Paul told Philemon that although Onesimus was unprofitable in the past, now he would be genuinely an Onesimus (profitable one, v. 11).

So Paul sent Onesimus back to his master and urged the master to receive him as though he were Paul himself. Paul would have liked to have kept Onesimus with himself in Rome. Then Onesimus could have ministered to Paul. But Paul wouldn't do that without first clearing it with Philemon, lest it appear that he was coercing Philemon (vv. 12-14).

Paul suggested that perhaps Onesimus had run away for just a temporary departure, according to the purpose of God, that he might return forever. And, that he might return, not just as a servant, but more than that, as a beloved brother (vv. 15, 16).

Finally, Paul asked Philemon directly to receive Onesimus as though he were Paul himself (v. 17). Then Paul went a step farther and said that if Onesimus owed his master any debt, Philemon should charge that to the apostle. To show his sincerity Paul signed the statement with his own hand, which according to Roman law would make it a legally binding contract (vv. 18, 19).

Picture yourself in Philemon's living room. Put yourself in Philemon's shoes. Seated across from you is your runaway slave, Onesimus. He sits there, apprehensive that you as a Roman citizen may exercise your right and have him put to death for his crime. He also sits there hoping that you as a Christian brother will find it in your heart to forgive him and take him back.

Next to him on the sofa is Tychicus, another brother in Christ. He has come with Onesimus all the way from Paul's presence in Rome. He has handed you the letter and also sits waiting to see what you will do.

Your sense of justice and maybe even fleshly revenge tugs at your heart. It tells you to execute Onesimus according to the law of the land.

But on the other hand, should not you forgive even as God for Christ's sake has forgiven you? Should not you make peace with this runaway slave even as God has made peace with you by the blood of Jesus Christ?

Your mind's eye leaps the miles beyond the sofa and you envision Paul sitting in his house in Rome next to a Roman soldier. You see him contemplating what you will do. He is praying to the Lord that people might see the working of Christ in your life. You want to let Paul have joy and refresh his heart in the Lord by doing what he requests.

Your struggle is real and yet you know what you will do. "Yes, I will forgive you!"

And then comes the rap at the door. That reporter is looking for more details.

2 Forgiven!

Verse to Memorize

Ephesians 4:32—"And be ye kind one to another, tenderhearted, forgiving one another, even as God for Christ's sake hath forgiven you."

Daily Bible Readings

Monday—What Love!—Luke 7:36-50
Tuesday—Perfect Sacrifice—Hebrews 10:1-14
Wednesday—"Father, Forgive Them"—Luke 23:24-34
Thursday—Just Like Jesus—Acts 7:51-60
Friday—Forgive Your Brother—Matthew 18:21-35
Saturday—This Takes Faith—Luke 17:1-5
Sunday—Love Is Greater—1 Corinthians 13

Search and Ponder

1. If the death of Jesus Christ was of sufficient value to pay for the sins of the world, then Who must He have been (Acts 20:28)? _____

2. When God forgives a person, does He "forgive but never forget" (Jer. 31:34)? _____

3. What similarity can you find between Romans 5:8 and Luke 23:34? _____

_____

4. Jesus taught that one who has been forgiven much will have much love for the one who forgave (Luke 7:40-43, 47). How much has God forgiven you? How have you responded with love to Him for His forgiveness? _____

_____

_____

5. Stephen followed Christ by seeking forgiveness for those who were killing him. How could Stephen do such a hard thing? (See Acts 7:54-60.)

_____

6. What is the standard by which one Christian is to forgive another (Eph. 4:32)? _____

_____

7. Jesus told of a much-forgiven servant who was unwilling to forgive someone who owed him a little (Matt. 18:21-35). How do our offenses against God compare with others' offenses against us? ____

_____

Then how should we forgive others? _____

_____

8. Describe the healing you have seen when Christians forgive one another. _____

_____

9. Is there someone you should forgive? _____

_____

10. Is there someone whose forgiveness you should seek? _____

Bible Portion to Read   Philemon 1-25

A certain creditor had two debtors. The one owed him 500 days' wages and the other only 50. Neither of the debtors had anything with which to pay. The creditor forgave both of them.

Jesus concluded that story by saying, "Tell me therefore, which of them will love him most?" (see Luke 7:41, 42).

The book of Philemon illustrates the very basic Christian truth of forgiveness. Paul did not use the word "forgive" as he wrote to Philemon, but the concept is abundantly clear in his writing. Philemon must not follow the trends of his day by executing his returning runaway. Rather, he was to receive Onesimus as he would receive Paul himself. He was to forgive Onesimus.

God's graciousness toward a sinner lifts the concept of forgiveness to an even greater height. The enormity of sin makes God's forgiveness shine with splendor.

The Background of Forgiveness

God's concept of a lost person shocks us because it is so different from our concept. The holy, righteous, pure God of the universe fully sees the reality of sin.

We humans often evaluate ourselves by com-

We humans often evaluate ourselves by community standards or by the average of the group of which we are a part. God evaluates us by the perfection of His own nature.

munity standards or by the average of the group of which we are a part. God evaluates us by the perfection of His own nature. He sees that "all have sinned, and come short of the glory of God (Rom. 3:23). He says that we were conceived in iniquity (Ps. 51:5); that is, we inherited sinfulness from our parents. Therefore, we possess an evil heart (Mark 7:21-23) and are full of unrighteousness (Rom. 1:28-32). We stand before the Judge of the universe, and His wrath abides on us, just waiting to be poured out against us (John 3:18, 36).

Here, forgiveness enters the picture. God's forgiveness releases us from the death penalty of sin. It pardons us and dismisses the charges brought by our sin. Only God could forgive us because our offenses have been against Him. David spoke correctly, "Against thee, thee only, have I sinned, and done this evil in thy sight" (Ps. 51:4).

The Basis of Forgiveness

How can a just and righteous God forgive sin? He can forgive humans because His own Son has paid the penalty in our place! When Christ shed His blood at Calvary, He bore our sins in His own body on the tree (1 Pet. 2:24). He suffered the death penalty of sin so that God could forgive us that penalty. God's grace is infinitely rich, and He forgives those who come to Him by faith in Christ in a measure which parallels that infinitely rich grace.

God's forgiveness applies to all our sins, for He tells us that those in Christ are under no condemning judgment whatsoever. It avails for our sinful deeds (Rom. 4:7) and for the sinful thoughts of our heart (Acts 8:22).

God's forgiveness is received when a person receives Christ as Savior. This is taught by several Scriptures. Paul was sent to the Gentiles "to open their eyes, and to turn them from darkness to light, and from the power of Satan unto God, that they may receive forgiveness of sins, and inheritance among them [who] are sanctified by faith that is in me" (Acts 26:18).

When a person is saved, he is placed into a living union or relationship with Christ, and forgiveness comes to those "in" Christ (Eph. 1:7). The Scriptures connect forgiveness to repentance, which is part of saving faith (Acts 5:31). Acts 10:43 contains a clear statement: "To him give all the prophets witness, that through his name whosoever believeth in him shall receive remission of sins."

Forgiveness is the precious possession of everyone who is God's child by being born again into the family of God (John 1:12, 13).

Reminders of Forgiveness

Forgiveness plagues all of us, not just the elderly. That's why God gave us so many reminders in His Word. Not only does His Word teach forgiveness over and over, but we are continually reminded of God's forgiveness by both of the ordinances which God has given to the local church.

Baptism speaks of forgiveness, according to

Acts 2:38. Some have sorely misunderstood this verse. It reads, "Then Peter said unto them, Repent, and be baptized every one of you in the name of Jesus Christ for the remission of sins. . . ." The key is the word "for." It, like the Greek word it translates, means "because of" or "on the basis of." We might say of a man, "He was sent to prison for murder," by which we mean he was imprisoned on the basis of what he had done; he had murdered. Peter told people to be baptized on the basis of the repentance and forgiveness which they had already experienced. Water baptism is a personal testimony of one's salvation and a reminder of the forgiveness which God gave the individual at the time of his salvation.

The Lord's Supper also speaks of forgiveness. The night before His death, Christ instituted the Lord's Supper observance. He explained the symbolism of the cup with these words, "For this is my blood of the new testament, which is shed for many for the remission [forgiveness] of sins" (Matt. 26:28).

A periodic communion service reminds us of God's forgiveness and the basis of that forgiveness, His shed blood. God blesses our hearts with encouragement as we diligently remember His forgiveness of us when we observe baptism or the Lord's Supper.

The Proclamation of Forgiveness

Those forgiven by God are to proclaim His forgiveness to others. Luke's account of the Great Commission records Christ's words: "That repentance and remission [forgiveness] of sins should be preached in his name among all nations, beginning at Jerusalem. And ye are witnesses of these things" (Luke 24:47, 48).

Paul confessed that God commanded us to preach Christ as the Judge of all men and "that through his name whosoever believeth in him shall receive remission [forgiveness] of sins" (Acts 10:42, 43). Paul set an example of obedience to that command. He stood in the synagogue at Antioch of Pisidia on his very first missionary journey. He read from the Old Testament and then preached to those assembled that Jesus was the promised Deliverer: "Be it known unto you therefore, men and brethren, that through this man is preached unto you the forgiveness of sins: and by him all that believe are justified from all things, from which ye could not be justified by the law of Moses" (Acts 13:38, 39).

You and I, as messengers of the gospel, are proclaimers of forgiveness. Forgiveness will attract a person more strongly than will a million-dollar giveaway, when that person has come to realize his sinfulness and dire need of God's forgiveness. On the other hand, one who has no sense of his sinfulness will not be impressed by God's offer of forgiveness.

We must be tools in God's hands to show people their sinful condition. We can pray that God will lead us to use the Scriptures that they need. We can pray that God will open their spiritual eyes to understand and accept His evaluation of their iniquity. We can pray that God will even use our righteous daily living to illustrate the difference between the ways of the world and the ways of God. And then with loving boldness we must share the message of the gospel, that Christ died for our sins. The more precious forgiveness is to us, the more persuasively we can present it to others.

The Practice of Forgiveness

Those forgiven by God not only proclaim His forgiveness but must also practice forgiveness toward other people. We are to follow the pattern of our Savior, Who prayed from the cross, "Father, forgive them; for they know not what they do" (Luke 23:34).

Peter once asked the Lord how many times he must forgive a brother who sinned against him. He offered to forgive seven times, which was no small ideal. Jesus replied that seven times would not be adequate, and He set the requirement at 70 times 7, or 490 times (Matt. 18:21, 22). In other words, the Lord said we must not limit our forgiveness of others to a calculated number of times.

Our Lord proceeded to illustrate His teaching with a story. He told about a king who had a servant. The servant owed that king an amount that was in the millions. When the king demanded payment, the servant fell down and begged that he be given an extension; he promised to pay if the time would just be made long enough. We read that the king took compassion upon him and even forgave him the entire debt of millions. Then this forgiven servant refused to forgive another man who owed him comparatively little.

You and I, as Christians, are instructed to be "forgiving one another, even as God for Christ's sake hath forgiven you" (Eph. 4:32). Certainly, like the servant of the king, we have been forgiven much. What people do to us here on earth is relatively small compared to what we have done to violate God's holiness. If He can forgive us, then we should forgive others.

Knowing that I *should be* forgiving is one

thing. *Wanting to be* forgiving is something else. And *actually forgiving* from the heart is more difficult still. How can I forgive others?

You and I need love, or caring concern, for others if we are to be forgiving. Forgiveness will spring from a heart that really loves the other person (1 Cor. 13:4-8). If we genuinely want what is best for another, we will not harbor an unforgiving spirit or seek revenge. A loving attitude is a spring sending forth a stream of forgiveness.

You and I also need faith if we are to be forgiving. The Lord told His disciples that if their brother should trespass against them and repent, they should forgive him. And even if he should do that seven times in one day, they should forgive him. The disciples' response was, "Lord, Increase our faith" (Luke 17:5). The disciples realized such forgiveness is not natural. A person must have faith to believe that forgiveness is God's will, or that one will never call upon the Lord in faith to help him.

It is a great blessing to be forgiven by God. The Scriptures say, "Blessed are they whose iniquities are forgiven, and whose sins are covered. Blessed is the man to whom the Lord will not impute sin" (Rom. 4:7, 8).

It's also a blessing to be forgiven by your fellow Christian. Following the principle that it is more blessed to give than to receive, it is a great blessing to give forgiveness to others. Do you and I fully appreciate the forgiveness that God has given us? And are we working on forgiving others?

3 Godly Leadership

Verse to Memorize

Titus 1:16—"They profess that they know God; but in works they deny him, being abominable, and disobedient, and unto every good work reprobate."

Daily Bible Readings

Monday—Welcome to Titus—
   2 Corinthians 7:1-6, 13-15
Tuesday—A Caring Partner—
   2 Corinthians 8:16-24
Wednesday—Godly Leaders—1 Timothy 3:1-13
Thursday—Godly Leadership—Acts 20:17-38
Friday—Ungodly Leaders—Ezekiel 34:1-10
Saturday—Saved by Faith—Galatians 3:1-13
Sunday—Faith and Works—James 2:14-26

Search and Ponder

1. God comforted Paul by Titus' arrival (2 Cor. 7:6). Have you ever been comforted by the visit of another Christian? _____ Did you see that visit as God's comfort? _____ To whom could

your visit be God's comfort? _____

2. Tears flowed as Paul said goodbye to the Ephesian elders, following a three-year ministry. As Paul left, he commended them into the care of two powerful agents (Acts 20:32). What were they? _____

3. What did Paul say God cannot do (Titus 1:2)? _____

4. With God all things are possible (Matt. 19:26). Then why is it said that God *cannot* lie? __

_____

5. What is an "elder," and what is a "bishop" (Titus 1:5, 7)? _____

_____

6. What word would you use to summarize all the qualities for church leaders in Titus 1:6-9? _____

7. To whom does Paul refer when he speaks of people belonging to "the circumcision" (Titus 1:10)? _____

8. Paul referred to a non-Christian prophet who had analyzed the Cretan culture, and the apostle agreed with one of his statements (Titus 1:12). The statement declared that _____

_____ .

9. Summarize similarities between Titus 1:16 and Matthew 7:15-20. _____

_____

_____

10. Would you say that ungodly leaders, such as Titus faced (Titus 1:10-16), can be found in professing Christianity today? _____ Explain

your answer. _____

_____

**Bible
Portion
to Read**   Titus 1:1-16

Suppose a veteran missionary had taken you as his companion to open a pioneer field. The gospel had borne fruit, and believers were now scattered throughout several cities. Then the missionary moved away and left *you* to guide these new Christians in their growth and to establish them into local churches. Wouldn't it be wonderful to get a letter of encouragement and instruction from the absent missionary? You would treasure that letter as a true lifesaver.

I imagine that's how Titus felt when this letter arrived from Paul. Our study of the book of Philemon showed that Paul had been imprisoned when he wrote that book, but he anticipated being released. Apparently he was released, and in his travels he proclaimed the gospel on the island of Crete. The new converts there were not yet established into organized churches when Paul departed. So he left Titus in Crete to complete the founding of the churches and to ordain the leaders of those churches (Titus 1:5). The epistle to Titus contains Paul's encouragement and instruction to Titus for his demanding task.

Now trade places for a moment. Suppose you must write a letter to young Titus, guiding him in his task. You tell yourself you want to

> Good works give a Christian the knowledge/
> assurance that he really does know God. The
> absence of good works indicates the person's
> profession of faith in Christ is a lie.

emphasize one central idea. You must drive
home a single point. What will it be?

Paul chose the theme of godliness. We might
use the words "holiness" or "righteousness"
instead. Paul wanted the Christians of Crete
to be godly in their character and in their
behavior. This letter to Titus sounds much like
the book of James, as both epistles stress the
importance of good works. The true believer
will have good works as the result of salvation.

A classic passage on works and salvation is
Ephesians 2:8-10. Verses 8 and 9 clearly state
that good works do *not* bring about salvation.
A person is saved by grace through faith and
apart from works. In fact, the unsaved person
does not even do anything that God would
consider to be good works (Rom. 3:12). However,
after one is saved by faith in Christ, the picture
totally changes. Ephesians 2:10 hastens to add
that one who has become a Christian by faith
alone must put good works on the agenda of
his life. Somehow verse 10 is forgotten all too
often.

The Holy Spirit nailed down this matter of
a Christian's good works when he moved John
to write, "And [by this] we do know that we
know him, if we keep his commandments. He
that saith, I know him, and keepeth not his
commandments, is a liar, and the truth is not
in him" (1 John 2:3, 4). Good works give a Christian the knowledge/assurance that he really does

know God. The absence of good works indicates the person's profession of faith in Christ is a lie.

The book of Titus shows us specifically what good works are and how they fit into the life of a Christian. Sounds exciting!

Greetings

Today we begin our letters with a two-word greeting, "Dear _____." Paul followed the custom of his day by writing an extended greeting which occupies four verses. Three verses describe the sender, Paul; one verse describes the receiver, Titus.

Notice two contrasting descriptions of Paul; he was both a servant and an apostle (Titus 1:1). A servant was a slave who had willingly surrendered his freedom to spend himself meeting the needs of his master. In the same breath Paul called himself an apostle. The apostles of Christ were an exclusive group. They had been selected and commissioned by the Lord Himself. They possessed miracle-working power as a credential. They were people of honor and authority. Paul saw himself as a humble servant with great authority from God. Paul had a healthy self-image.

"Self-image" has become a household word. The Christian may wonder how he should view himself. God's Word gives the answer as though it were written this year. Every person who knows Christ must not think of himself more highly than he ought to think (Rom. 12:3). A caution against pride is well placed, for pride so permeates the fallen thoughts. However, the Holy Spirit did not let Paul stop at that point.

"Think soberly, according as God hath dealt to every man the measure of faith," Paul instructed (Rom. 12:3). A proper self-concept for the Christian involves a realistic evaluation of what God has dealt to that person. The context of Romans 12 speaks of the grace gifts that God gives to His own. Every member of Christ's Body receives a special endowment from the Lord. To deny that gift is to deny the Giver.

The Christian views himself as God views him. He sees himself as gifted by God and so avoids the pride of self-sufficiency and the despair of worthlessness. That is realistic and Biblical.

Godly Leaders

"Everything rises or falls with leadership" is an often-quoted saying. We are not surprised that Paul began his letter about godliness at the point of leadership. If the Cretan churches would be godly, they must have godly leadership. The same is true of our churches.

Titus 1:6-9 lists qualifications of godliness for the church leaders. Read through those verses. As you think on these qualities, you notice they are spiritual. They are either character qualities or behavioral qualities that display Christian maturity. God desires godly leaders, and a church needs godly leaders.

Too often churches think primarily in terms of professional expertise and personal charisma when they think of pastoral qualifications. Those areas are important and have their place when considering who is best equipped for the task. But the basic and absolutely essential qualities for church leadership are spiritual. Abilities and charm, apart from spiritual maturity, operate on

the level of the flesh and do not accomplish the
purposes of God. We must ever insist upon these
major things which God Himself has required.

New Testament churches which select their
own pastors by vote of the membership must have
a membership who know what to look for in a
pastor. No man will be perfect in all these
qualities or even in one of them. But every pastor
must show a recognizable level of maturity in
these things, and he should be making continual
progress in them.

These qualities are necessary for a pastor for
several reasons. For one thing, he must lead his
people into these qualities. These qualities are
goals for all Christians. Too often people are
content to demand Christian character of the
church leaders while excusing themselves from
the same rigorous standards. As you study Titus
1:6-9, identify one or more of these qualities in
which you need improvement, and ask God daily
to help you strengthen them in your life.

Physical violence threatens. It assaults many in
their bodies, and it assaults vastly more in their
minds as they view it in the media. Modern
television programming emphasizes physical
force as a common solution to problems. Fights
and weapons appear as a basic ingredient of
prime time. Today's youth suffer the inescapable
influence of these portrayals of violence. Even a
few pastors have been known to attack others.

God forbids the pastor to hit others physically.

33

Moses had a problem in this area. He struck the Egyptian; he crushed the tablets of commandments; and he later struck the rock when God told him to merely speak to it. After these repeated "strikes," God refused to let him enter the Promised Land.

A missionary family, traveling from one island to another in the South Pacific, sailed into a fierce storm. Their boat capsized and broke apart. Crushing waves swept away two of their precious children, but the parents and two other children finally washed onto shore, barely alive and clinging to shattered pieces of their boat. They were spared because they held fast to floating debris.

The pastor likewise must cling to God's faithful Word (Titus 1:9). The highest waves of false teaching or opposition cannot sink the pastor who holds fast to the faithful Word of God.

Ungodly Leaders

Have you heard someone say, "Our town is a very difficult field for the gospel"? Have you ever felt that way about your town? Possibly so. I imagine the Cretans might have felt that way about their island (Titus 1:10–16).

Crete had a host of door-to-door religious leaders who claimed to know God (v. 11). They were effective in getting others to follow them. They may even have had professional expertise and personal charisma. But they denied God by their behavior, showing that they were not truly saved. Their message was vain and deceptive.

Paul's words perfectly describe today's scene. Religious leaders abound who do not submit themselves to God's rules, who seek to add meritorious works to God's grace, who speak forth great volumes of words but without real meaning, and who deceive multitudes away from God and into following erroneous humans. Their underlying motivation is money. Paul could have written these verses to our generation.

What should the churches do? Human reasoning might propose a strategy built upon Christians who were more talented and more persuasive than the false teachers. But God's strategy was built upon men with the spiritual qualities just studied. God would use people who were living a godly life and holding fast to the faithful Word.

The godly leaders would minister that faithful Word. They were to rebuke the false teachers sharply (v. 13). The purpose of the rebuke was to make the false leaders become "sound in the faith." "The faith" refers to Christian truth or the doctrines held by true Christians.

The conflict between the godly and ungodly leaders was not a conflict of flesh and blood; rather, it was a spiritual warfare. Therefore, the godly leaders, dressed in the whole armor of God, were to take up the Sword of the Spirit, which is the Word of God, and go forth to battle. The Cretan churches dealt with false teachers by means of godly leaders wielding the Word of God

Paul's final description of the ungodly leaders is chilling. They professed to know God when they did not (v. 16). Such false profession, believed by many, made them more effective in their evil work. But the many who uncritically accepted their profession of faith should have known better, for their works clearly denied the Lord and thus proved their profession of faith to be false. More about this will be found in the next chapter.

4 A Godly Life-style

Verse to Memorize

Titus 2:1—"But speak thou the things which become sound doctrine."

Daily Bible Readings

Monday—Good Doctrine—1 Timothy 4:6–16

Tuesday—Holiness—Leviticus 27:9–34

Wednesday—Much Wine—Proverbs 23:19–35

Thursday—Family Guidelines—Ephesians 5:21—6:4

Friday—Spiritual Sacrifices—Hebrews 13:10–21

Saturday—Facing the Fire—1 Corinthians 3:1–17

Sunday—Bosses and Workers—Ephesians 6:5–9; 1 Peter 2:18–25

Search and Ponder

1. Jogging and exercise programs are sweeping our land. Is there profit in such exercise? _____

What is more profitable than physical exercise (see 1 Tim. 4:8)? _____

How do you apportion time to these two areas? ___

___

2. What do you know of the Bible's teaching concerning alcoholic beverages (without doing research)? ___

___

3. God's guidelines for family relationships contain specific directions for husbands and wives (Eph. 5:21-33). What is a husband's responsibility to his wife? ___

And a wife's responsibility to her husband? ___

___

Should the married person force his/her spouse to fulfill their responsibility? ___

___

4. Church-age saints offer spiritual sacrifices rather than animal sacrifices. What are some of our spiritual sacrifices (Heb. 13:15, 16)? ___

___

5. How could you as an employee practice the principles for workers found in Ephesians 6:5-8 and 1 Peter 2:18-25? ___

___

6. How could you as an employer practice the principles for masters found in Ephesians 6:9 and Colossians 4:1? ___

___

7. Carnality has always been a problem in local

churches. What definite evidence revealed carnality in the church at Corinth (1 Cor. 3:3)? _____

_____

8. What is some ministry in which retired Christians should be involved (Titus 2:2-5)? _____

_____

9. What guidelines does Titus 2:4-8 give to younger Christians? _____

_____

10. What is the relationship between good works and salvation? _____

_____

_____

**Bible
Portion
to Read**   Titus 2:1–10

The infamy of old, reclusive Mr. Grumps had spread even beyond his own neighborhood. His closet bulged with children's balls which he had snatched from his yard before their owners could climb the fence to retrieve them. The neighborhood kids hated him and did their best to treat him as meanly as he expected them to.

When two well-meaning Christian children attempted to invite Mr. Grumps to services at their church, they were treated to a slamming door. They decided to demonstrate the love of Christ by cutting Mr. Grumps overgrown grass for him. At first he rejected their offer as some plot and even threatened them. But finally he softened.

When they completed the job and refused payment, he asked why they had done it. They seized the opportunity and began an effective witness for Christ. Their experience displayed how a godly life-style can make the gospel attractive, just as hypocrisy can turn people away from Christ.

Titus 2:1-10 is one of the most practical sections of God's Word. It addresses young and old, men and women and servants with instructions for godly living. You will find that these verses operate right where the rubber meets the road.

The Relationship of Behavior and Belief

Some things just go together—mashed potatoes and gravy, bacon and eggs, ham and cheese, belief and behavior. One's beliefs regulate one's behavior. The book of Titus shows that wrong beliefs lead to wrong behavior, while right beliefs result in right behavior.

In our last chapter we saw godly leaders and ungodly leaders. The ungodly leaders opposed sound doctrine. Their teaching was vain, for they adopted fables and the commandments of men. They turned from the truth. But not only were their beliefs wrong, their behavior was wrong as well. In their works they denied God, being abominable, disobedient and reprobate (or worthless) for every good work. Wrong beliefs led to wrong behavior.

You will notice that the ungodly leaders professed to know God (Titus 1:16). They were not part of some obviously heathen group. They

> When a person's life does not correspond with his claim to be saved, we should have urgent concern for his soul and not casually assume that he is merely backslidden. He may be on his way to hell.

claimed to know Christ, although they really did not. How did discerning believers discover that these teachers were false professors? They looked at the behaviors of the ungodly leaders and saw that in their works they denied God.

Jesus Christ taught, "By their fruits ye shall know them" (Matt. 7:16, 20). When a person professes faith in Christ and then begins to develop in his obedience to Christ's commands, the evidence of his life points to a genuine conversion (1 John 2:3, 5). But when a person professes faith in Christ and he does not develop in obedience to Christ's commands, the evidence of his life points to a false profession (1 John 2:4).

We humans cannot know precisely the heart condition of another. Only God knows for sure who is saved and who is lost. But when a person's life does not correspond with his claim to be saved, we should have urgent concern for his soul and not casually assume that he is merely backslidden. He may be on his way to hell.

The godly leaders believed sound doctrines. They held fast to God's faithful Word. They knew sound doctrine so well that they could use it in ministering to others. But not only was their doctrine good, their behavior was godly as well. They restrained internal urges to flare up in anger. They kept their minds from the dulling effects of alcohol. They loved their wives and led their children well. In fact, they were blameless. Sound doctrine led to a godly life-style.

The Regulations for Godly Behavior

A pastor was driving along one night when he spotted a parked car. The car belonged to a young Christian who was still struggling with a long-standing alcohol habit. Just around the corner was a bar. The pastor pulled over, prayed and went into the bar, searching for the young Christian. The shocked young Christian greeted the pastor with these words, "*You* shouldn't be in a place like this!"

We expect high standards of godly living from the leadership of the church. But sometimes we forget that the same standards apply to every Christian and should be the goal of each one of us. We must not allow ourselves the "luxury" of lower levels of godliness just because we do not hold an office in the church. The New Testament permits no such distinction between the "clergy" and the "laity."

A godly life-style or righteous living is for every Christian. Paul gave Titus examples of a godly life-style for five categories of people. He mentioned the aged men, the aged women, young women, young men and servants.

Our popular designation "middle age" must have been unknown in Paul's day, so perhaps you will have a difficult time deciding to which group you belong. In that case, you may want to consider both the young and aged groups. At any rate, realize that the Holy Spirit has written very practical directions in our Scripture portion for today, and seek to incorporate this teaching into your behavior.

Aged men. Six characteristics are given for aged men (Titus 2:2). They must be sober or sober-minded. Their years of experience have taught them not to get carried away by grandiose schemes or insurmountable difficulties. They have conscious control of their faculties and a clear perspective for wisely evaluating situations.

The older man is to be grave, or dignified. He can have fun, but he knows well that life is serious business. There is a time to rejoice and a time to be serious.

The older Christian is to be temperate. He has learned the futility and deceptiveness of the world's values. He sees things from God's perspective, noting what is of eternal value and what is of only temporal value.

The older Christian man is to be sound (strong) in faith, love and patience. By virtue of the months and years he has walked with God daily, he will have a strong personal confidence in God and be well-taught in the truth of the Word. He will have learned to walk in love, caring for the welfare of others even as the Savior cared. He will have developed unswerving commitment to Christ, no matter what happens.

Aged women. Four characteristics are given to aged women (v. 3). Their behavior should become holiness, or to be very literal, their behavior should be proper for a priest. A priest's behavior is primarily that of offering sacrifices. The aged women should be experts in offering spiritual sacrifices to God.

They must not be false accusers. The tongue is very difficult to control. However, it can be controlled by God's grace. The Proverbs contain much wisdom about the tongue. The tongue is powerful to hurt and to heal (Prov. 12:18). Such a potent force must be used to build up rather than to tear down. The mature Christian woman is expected to have learned control of the tongue.

She must not be given to much wine. She must not look to alcohol to give "relief" and make her feel better. The strength for living does not come in a bottle.

Older women are to be teachers of good things. Having discovered what things are good and how those things can be developed in life, they seek to teach younger women what they have learned over many years.

Young women. The young Christian woman is to love her husband and her children (v. 4). This prescription must have been written with us in mind. The forces getting center stage today elevate a woman's personal pleasure and personal fulfillment, which supposedly can be found only away from the husband and the home. If God wants a young Christian woman to love her family and be a homemaker, don't you think He can give her a true sense of fulfillment in doing His will? What could be more rewarding than molding young minds and lives.

The young woman must also be discreet (same word as "temperate" in 2:2), chaste and good (v. 5). The beauty of a pure, sober-minded woman whose life overflows with good works must be a sweet fragrance to God, even as it is to her Christian friends.

Young men. The only requirement mentioned for young men is that they be sober-minded (v. 6). However, Titus was in this group, and the things commanded of him (vv. 7–9) could be followed by all young men with great profit.

Servants. The principles of master-servant relationships correlate to employee-employer relationships. As you study verses 9 and 10, think of how you could practice these commands with your boss or your workers.

The Reasons for Godly Behavior

God often gives us reasons for His requirements. He laced the requirements for godly living with several reasons, showing us the practical advantage (not to mention the spiritual advantage) of doing as He says.

The young women were told that when they behaved as they should, then the Word of God would not be blasphemed (v. 5). The implication is that should they misbehave, the Word of God would be blasphemed. No serious Christian wants to bring an attack upon the Word of God!

Titus was told that his proper behavior would result in the enemies of the gospel having no evil thing to say of him (v. 8). We all dislike personal criticism. But something more important is at stake. The world tends to judge Christ by Christians. So if our behavior is above reproach, we have spared the Lord criticism.

Servants (employees) were told that their right behavior would adorn the doctrine of God our Savior (v. 10). Their godly life-style would show the gospel to be genuine and effective. They would be presenting the good news of salvation in an attractive package of their own good behavior.

A godly life-style aids evangelism by removing objections against the Word and against Christians, and by demonstrating that the gospel leads to an attractive life.

H-1-84

5 Where Godliness Comes From

Verse to Memorize

Titus 2:14—"Who gave himself for us, that he might redeem us from all iniquity, and purify unto himself a peculiar people, zealous of good works."

Daily Bible Readings

Monday—Amazing Grace—Romans 5:12-21

Tuesday—Deny Ungodliness— Ephesians 4:17-32

Wednesday—A Holy God—Psalm 99

Thursday—Anchoring Hope—Hebrews 6:10-20

Friday—Zealous for Good Works—2 Corinthians 9:1-9

Saturday—Obey Government—Romans 13:1-7; 1 Peter 2:13-17

Sunday—Past Behavior—1 Peter 4:1-11

Search and Ponder

1. When humans take an oath, they sware by something greater than themselves. When God made an oath to Abraham, by what/whom did He

sware (Heb. 6:13)? _____

2. People hold many different views concerning the purpose of human government. According to Romans 13:1-7 and 1 Peter 2:13 and 14, what is the God-intended role of government? _____

3. Governments "bear the sword" (Rom. 13:4). What does that mean? _____

4. How extensively must the Christian obey the government (Rom. 13:1-7; 1 Pet. 2:13, 14)? _____

_____

What about obeying speed limits? _____

_____

5. What reasons does God give for our obedience to the government (Rom. 13:1-7; 1 Pet. 2:13, 14)?

_____

_____

6. How would you distinguish between our culture's idea of hope and the Christian idea of hope? _____

_____

7. What "subjects" does the grace of God teach us (Titus 2:11-13)? _____

_____

_____

8. For what is the Christian to be looking (Titus 2:13)? _____

9. According to Titus 2:14 for what two reasons did Christ die? _____

10. We who are now Christians were sometimes (complete Titus 3:3) " _____

_____
_____
_____."

**Bible
Portion
to Read**   Titus 2:11—3:3

Six-year-old Mary arrived home from school one day with a question: "Mommy, where did I come from?" After her mother had spent several minutes explaining the growth and birth of babies, Mary exclaimed with a puzzled look, "That's strange, Susie said she came from New York!"

We have been learning about godly behavior from our study of Titus. Where does godliness come from? Does it come from strong self-determination, or positive thinking, or some mysterious experience?

The Basis for Godliness

"The grace of God that bringeth salvation hath appeared to all men" (Titus 2.11). This is a reference to the first coming of Jesus Christ. His coming was motivated by the grace of God. When He was here, He demonstrated the grace of God in more detail than ever before (John 1:17), so it is proper to refer to the Person of Jesus Christ as "the grace of God."

When Christ came, He brought salvation. That salvation has several different aspects. His salvation saves from the penalty of sin so that all the condemning judgment of God against sin is removed. Christ's salvation also saves from the enslaving power of sin. Lost people have sin as their master. They think they are free to do whatever they want, and in a sense that is true. The problem is that what they want to do is what the devil wants them to do (John 8:44), and so they are unwitting dupes of Satan.

There is a progression to the bondage of sin. Some sins get such a grip on the human will or body or mind that they become obviously enslaving. How tragic when a person in such slavery to sin still protests that he is free. How tragic that he prefers his abject condition to the limitations of God's Word.

The salvation of Jesus Christ sets one free from sin to serve God: "If the Son therefore shall make you free, ye shall be free indeed" (John 8:36). "But now being made free from sin, and become servants to God, ye have your fruit unto holiness, and the end everlasting life" (Rom. 6:22). All life is service. One spends his days serving his Creator or serving the arch-enemy of his soul.

Have you ever stopped to consider what true freedom is? The old nature defines freedom as the absence of restraints, but real freedom is the ability to do what you were designed to do.

Suppose a train were to look longingly at cows grazing in a meadow and wish it could be free from the constraints of two steel ribbons. Give the train its wish, and immediately it would sink to its axles and become totally immobile. Leave it on the tracks, and it is free to pull valuables and men from point to point, fulfilling its intended purpose.

A human being is God's creation, designed to bring glory to God and enjoy Him forever. Keep him on the path of righteousness, and he fulfills his purpose and experiences the greatest sense of satisfaction possible. Give him his vain wish to be free from God's restraints, and he immediately sinks into the mire of sinful entanglements.

Jesus Christ, the Savior, lifts sinners out of the pit and sets them upon the solid rock. Then He enables them to be fruitful in life. The fruit of godliness can occur only as one abides in Him, the Vine. Without Him we can do nothing that God considers good or godly (John 15:4, 5).

More Godly Behavior

Paul's letter to Titus has described many godly behaviors. The requirements for church leaders, for men and women of different ages and for servants reveal many things God wants His children to do or not to do. Titus 2:12—3:2 contains more godly actions. These verses first list general behaviors and then specific behaviors.

General behaviors. Christians must amputate certain practices (2:12). Ungodliness, a lack of reverence toward God, must be eliminated. Such is typical of the unsaved and causes the continual display of God's wrath (Rom. 1:18).

The future holds the great and terrible day of God's wrath. And yet Romans 1:18 teaches that God is constantly showing wrath against ungodliness. Why don't we recognize this display of God's activity? Precisely because it is always taking place. Things which occur with normal frequency we accept as the laws of nature, and we fail to see God's hand at work.

Ask any policeman if ungodliness brings trouble. Ask any pastor the same question. Anyone who works closely with people knows that ungodliness has accompanying difficulties. The rise of a terrible new disease primarily among a class of people who engage in unnatural and unseemly practices seems to be a current display of God's wrath against ungodliness.

Christians must also graft certain practices into their lives. While there are things to be denied, there are other things to be incorporated into life. Three words describe the proper way to live: "soberly," "righteously" and "godly." The word "godly" is the same word as "ungodly" except that the negative prefix is missing. The godly person holds God in high esteem and directs his life according to God's will.

Specific behaviors. Paul's epistle to Titus contains some specific directions for Christians in their relationship to the government and to the society in which they live (3:1).

The government's role would be radically varied if all people had their way. Some see the government primarily as the provider for the needy. Others see it as the solver of all problems. Still others view it as the protector of the nation. God, Who established human government, revealed His intended role for it. If you have not considered "Search and Ponder" question 2, do that now. It will direct you to God's view of government.

The Christian's responsibility toward the government is summarized in the words "submit" and "obey." Of course, obedience to human governments is not absolute, for they sometimes make requirements that specifically contradict God's claims upon life. In such cases, "We ought to obey God rather than men" (Acts 5:29). Remember, we will each give an accounting to God as to how we obeyed the government over us. Let us be careful not to stretch Acts 5:29 beyond the limits of application acceptable to God.

The Christian's responsibility toward society includes four items named in Titus 3:1 and 2. We must be ready to do good to all people. We are not to speak evil of any man. We are not to be brawlers who resort to physical violence to settle issues. On the other hand, we are to be gentle, which is a display of meekness.

Treating offensive people with gentleness tries one's soul. But the Christian has good reason to do so. Before he was saved he was "foolish, disobedient, deceived, serving [various] lusts and pleasures, living in malice and envy, hateful and hating one another" (Titus 3:3).

How did God treat the offending sinner who is now a Christian? With kindness and love! Therefore, as God's representative, the Christian should now treat unsaved people as God treated him when he was unsaved.

An Incentive for Godliness

Two appearings of Jesus Christ are mentioned in our text for today. He appeared once in history to provide salvation (2:11). That salvation redeems us from all iniquity. But it also was intended to revolutionize our manner of life here on earth. Christ died to purify unto Himself a people who obviously belong to Him and who zealously pursue good works (2:14).

Jesus Christ will yet appear in the future (2:13). This future appearing shines as a blessed hope. Certain descriptions are given of Jesus Christ as He will appear. These descriptions emphasize His character as it will be shown in the appearing that will fulfill the believer's hope.

Suppose a relative of yours from far away is coming to visit you. If he is known for his fun-loving ways you will plan for a good time when he arrives. If he is known as a meticulous person, you will spend time cleaning the house in preparation for his arrival. Your knowledge of his character governs your preparation for his arrival.

So it is with the believer and Jesus Christ. He is coming as the great God and as the Savior Who expects sanctified living and Who suffered crucifixion to enable His children to do it. Since we know He wants us to be pure and to be zealous of good works, those things should be our preparation for His arrival.

Godliness comes from Jesus Christ. His death made it possible. Abiding in Him makes godliness a reality in the life of a Christian. But just how important is godliness?

The message of godliness must be proclaimed. Titus was to speak these things. But mere speaking would not be enough. Some people would need more than just information, and so Titus was to exhort the Cretans in these matters. He was to urge them very strongly to be godly.

After much exhortation some people would still fail. Such people Titus was to rebuke, pointing out the error of their ways so they could see the difference between godliness and their own behavior.

Sadly, constant teaching, exhortation and even

rebuke would fail to impress some, because they would view Titus' message as merely his own opinions. And so he must teach, exhort and rebuke with authority. All the authority of God Himself stood behind the inspired words of Paul to Titus. Therefore the churches must take Titus quite seriously. He must not allow them to disregard his words.

These messages of godliness are urgent messages. The Cretan Christians needed to be impressed with them, and so do we. The blessed hope of Christ's return will be an extra blessing if we are prepared. "And now, little children, abide in him; that, when he shall appear, we may have confidence, and not be ashamed before him at his coming" (1 John 2:28).

6 Godliness in Action

Verse to Memorize

Titus 3:8—"This is a faithful saying, and these things I will that thou affirm constantly, that they which have believed in God might be careful to maintain good works. These things are good and profitable unto men."

Daily Bible Readings

Monday—God's Love—Romans 5:1-11

Tuesday—Not by Works—Galatians 2:11-21

Wednesday—Regeneration—John 3:1-13

Thursday—Justified by Grace—Romans 3:19-31

Friday—A Faithful Saying—1 Timothy 4:1-10

Saturday—Striving about the Law—Acts 15:1-11

Sunday—Be Not Unfruitful—John 15:1-8

Search and Ponder

1. What does Romans 5:1 mean when it says we have been "justified"? _____

_____

2. The believer can glory in tribulation because it is the first link in a four-link chain of cause and effect (Rom. 5:3, 4). List the four links. _____

_____

3. Why is it so amazing that Christ would die for us (Rom. 5:6-8)? _____

_____

4. Who will be justified by doing the good works of the law (Gal. 2:16)? _____

5. If it were possible to become righteous before God by keeping the law, then what would be true of Christ's death (Gal. 2:21)? _____

6. Instead of justifying people, the law brings a knowledge of _____ (Rom. 3:20).

7. Relate 1 Timothy 4:1-5 to religious vegetarianism and to saying grace before meals. _____

_____

_____

8. How many things which God would consider fruitful can we do without a close relationship with Christ (John 15:5)? _____

9. Those who have believed in God should be careful to _____
(Titus 3:8).

10. Believers should learn to _____
(Titus 3:14).

**Bible
Portion
to Read**   Titus 3:4-15

You could see him any day of the week, trudging through the alleys with his wooden pushcart. Sadness covered his face like the dirt covered his ragged clothing. Like a bee gathering nectar, he went from one garbage can to another, drawing out salable materials.

The obituary said that he died of malnutrition and pneumonia in his unheated, Midwestern shack. It also said that investigators found over one hundred thousand dollars in cash hidden throughout his home. Incredible!

But then why do we Christians so often live subnormal lives when we have been blessed with all spiritual blessings in heavenly places in Christ (Eph. 1:3)? Titus 3 shows us godliness in action. We should be challenged to live godly in Christ by drawing upon our great spiritual resources.

Titus 3:4-15 divides into three sections, showing godliness in God's actions, in the actions of believers and in Titus' actions.

God's Actions

The prophet Habakkuk faced some serious struggles. He knew that God was a holy God, but he could not understand why God permitted so much sin to continue among the Israelites. He talked to God about it. God replied that He was going to deal with that sin, and He would use the Babylonians to chasten the Israelites.

Then Habakkuk faced an even greater struggle. How could God use people who were more wicked than the Israelites to chasten Israel? The Lord gave a lengthy answer and strengthened Habakkuk's faith to the point that he could proclaim: "Although the fig tree shall not blossom, neither shall fruit be in the vines; the labour of the olive shall fail, and the fields shall yield no [food]; the flock shall be cut off from the fold, and there shall be no herd in the stalls: Yet I will rejoice in the LORD, I will joy in the God of my salvation" (Hab. 3:17, 18).

How can a person have such faith in God's actions, even when they seem so wrong? He must be convinced that "the ways of the LORD are right" (Hos. 14:9). What God does *is* right.

God's attributes are infinitely perfect. His perfections make Him a perfect moral standard. Everything He does harmonizes perfectly with the total combination of His attributes.

God's actions are godly. Some of His godly actions are saving lost people, shedding His Holy Spirit upon them, and making them heirs (Titus 3:5-7).

God has acted in saving us. Every Christian knows this even if he knows little else. "Salvation" is a broad term in the Bible. It means deliverance. Paul described salvation in Titus 3:5 in terms of the washing of regeneration and renewing of the Holy Spirit.

The word "regeneration" means to be born again. Jesus and Nicodemus engaged in a detailed discussion of this concept (John 3). Jesus taught him that no one could enter the kingdom of God unless he had been made over by the Holy Spirit in such a drastic way that only "being born again" would adequately describe it. Nicodemus, you'll remember, became confused and wondered how such a thing as rebirth could be possible. Certainly regeneration is a supernatural, miraculous work of God.

Regeneration gives eternal life (Titus 3:5). It makes a person such a new creation in Christ that

God sits as the Judge of all creation. He keeps records of men's deeds, including offenses against Him. But when God saves a person, He imparts that person's sin to Christ and Christ's righteousness to that person.

old things pass away and all things become new. It includes cleansing from sin.

The popular secular proverb "Cleanliness is next to godliness" has been often repeated. Certainly moral cleanliness falls within the boundaries of godliness, and physical cleanliness was an Old Testament symbol of moral purification.

Sin defiles like a spot or blemish that man cannot remove. Only God could provide a cleansing agent powerful enough to remove the defilements of sin. And that He has done in the blood of Christ, the perfect Sacrifice for sin. Regeneration brings a washing from sin's defilement that leaves the born-again babe in Christ spotless.

God has acted in "justifying" us. This word may seem complicated, but it simply means to declare one righteous (v. 7). When the publicans justified God (Luke 7:29), they declared that God was righteous (which He is by nature). When God justifies a sinner, He declares that sinner righteous (which he is by virtue of Christ's righteousness being put to his account, 2 Cor. 5:21).

God sits as the Judge of all creation. He keeps records of men's deeds, including offenses against Him. But when God saves a person, He imputes that person's sin to Christ and Christ's righteousness to that person. Therefore God truly and accurately declares the saved sinner to be righteous. Believers have been justified, for their change in standing took place at the time they trusted in Christ.

God has acted in giving us the Holy Spirit. During Jesus' earthly ministry, the Holy Spirit dwelt *with* the disciples, but He was not dwelling *in* them (John 14:17). Jesus repeatedly promised such a new and fuller ministry of the Holy Spirit that it would be almost as if the Holy Spirit were coming for the first time.

The Holy Spirit did come in His new ministry on the day of Pentecost (Acts 2). He baptized the believers into the Body of Christ, forming that new spiritual organism. He took up permanent residence in every believer, just as Christ had said that He would be "in" them. Every believer is a temple of the Holy Spirit. Should a person not have the Holy Spirit in this Age, then that person must not be a saved child of God (Rom. 8:9).

The Holy Spirit also seals every believer, marking him as God's possession and protecting him. He also teaches believers (1 Cor. 2:10-13) and performs other ministries, such as being the guarantee that we will receive our heavenly inheritance (Eph. 1:14).

God has acted in making us heirs. The one who is joined to Christ by faith shares the future with Christ as a joint heir (Rom. 8:17). When the Christian arrives at his heavenly Home, he will take full possession of an inheritance which is incorruptible, undefiled and unfading (1 Pet. 1:4).

Saving us, justifying us, giving us the Spirit and making us heirs are four actions of God which conform to His nature and lie exclusively within His abilities. Such actions deserve to be called godly actions.

Believers' Actions

Repetition may be the best teaching tool. The Holy Spirit certainly repeated the message of godly behavior as He guided Paul to complete his letter to Titus.

Maintain good works. The exhortation to good works appears twice in the final verses of Titus (3:8, 14). Those who have believed in God must be careful to maintain good works. Some believers start well in their walk with God, but they lose their first love along the way, and good works become less and less prevalent in their lives. God's will is for *all* who have believed to maintain good works.

Note carefully the order. First, one must believe, for salvation is by grace through faith and not by works of righteousness which we have done. But those who have believed must then be careful to lead lives full of good works.

This teaching, although neglected by some today, is so important to God that Paul calls it a faithful saying and urges that it be constantly affirmed to God's people. Furthermore, believers benefit from it, for it is good and profitable to them.

Avoid the unprofitable and vain. Separation means keeping apart from all that is evil and keeping close to the Holy God. Christians walking the path of godliness find the road has warning signs against certain turnoffs. The pilgrim must avoid foolish questions, genealogies, contentions and strivings about the law (v. 9).

People arose in the early church who taught that righteousness before God could be obtained by doing works. Such works-righteousness heresy appeals to the sinful heart which would like to deserve at least some credit for its own salvation. At Crete this heresy took the form of keeping rules and counting on heritage. The true Christians must not get involved in that system.

Most cults and false religions today offer a works-righteousness system of salvation. Doing good, participating in rituals, belonging to a "Christian" family or being part of some supposedly lost tribe of Israel gains the adherent favor with God. True Christians must be separated from such systems.

Reject heretics. Heretics are those who have chosen doctrine which is contrary to sound doctrine, and who therefore cause divisions over doctrine because their followers disagree with those who hold the truth.

The Christian must reject heretics for they have turned aside from God; they are sinning, and their teaching shows them to be under condemnation by God. However, the Christian is to warn the heretic of his dangerous position, hoping that he will repent. In fact, two warnings must precede the rejection of the person who is a heretic (vv. 10, 11).

Titus' Actions

You will remember that Paul had assigned Titus to Crete and the establishment of the Cretan churches. In this letter Paul summoned Titus to his side (3:12). Paul had been freed from prison in Rome and had decided to spend the winter at Nicopolis; he desired Titus' presence there.

Titus was to leave Crete when either Artemas or Tychicus should arrive there from Paul. Whichever one Paul finally sent would take Titus' place so he could leave; the work he was doing would continue.

Titus was to give missionary support to the team of Zenas and Apollos (v. 13). Paul knew they would be coming to Crete, and Titus was to assist them in their travels for the gospel. Perhaps he arranged meetings and hospitality for them and encouraged the churches to contribute to their support. It is possible that these two missionaries were Paul's couriers to take his letter to Titus.

Finally Titus should give Paul's greetings to all those who loved him in the faith (v. 15). Those whose hearts were bound to Paul's around the great truths of Christ received his greetings.

You have now reached the end of our study in Titus. You recall that the book of Philemon taught us forgiveness, the beginning of the Christian life. Titus has emphasized godly living. Many general and specific godly behaviors have been presented. Hopefully, God has spoken to you about how you should live.

7 Faithful Servants

Verse to Memorize

2 Timothy 1:8—"Be not thou therefore ashamed of the testimony of our Lord, nor of me his prisoner: but be thou partaker of the afflictions of the gospel according to the power of God."

Daily Bible Readings

Monday—We're Not Gods—Acts 14:6-20

Tuesday—Welcome to Timothy—Acts 15:36—16:5

Wednesday—The Gospel Invades Ephesus—Acts 18:18-28

Thursday—Paul Revisits Ephesus—Acts 19:1-10

Friday—Burning Bad Books—Acts 19:11-22

Saturday—Angry Idol-makers—Acts 19:23—20:1

Sunday—Timothy, Paul's Messenger—1 Timothy 1:1-11

Search and Ponder

1. What evidence for the existence of God did Paul mention to the people of Lystra (Acts 14:17)? _____

2. Whom did Paul refuse to take on his second missionary trip, and why did Paul refuse (Acts 15:36–38)? _____

_____

3. The Ephesian Christians burned their magical arts books. What items should we as Christians consider destroying? _____

_____

4. What great thing took place after the Ephesians removed evil literature which had influenced their thinking (Acts 19:20)? _____

_____

5. How did Christianity impact the economy of Ephesus (Acts 19:23–27)? _____

_____

6. What specific impact could the spread of the gospel have on society in your town? _____

_____

7. Paul asked Timothy to stay at _____ and minister there (1 Tim. 1:3).

8. How was Timothy's tender heart evident in 2 Timothy 1:4? _____

9. Is it all right for a Christian man to cry?

_____

10. Have you ever felt ashamed of the testimony of our Lord or of a rejected fellow Christian? _____

**Bible
Portion
to Read**   2 Timothy 1:1–8

His troops fought long and hard that day, but they were no match for the enemy. By evening the army was in full retreat, trying desperately to save as many lives as possible in the rout. Suddenly enemy fire hit him and he was severely wounded. The time had come for his final statement. It was a request for somone to administer the coup de grace so he would not be captured alive. When no one would, King Saul took his own life.

Nearly a millennium later the apostle Paul faced death. The time had come for him to make his final statement. But what a difference! Paul's last written statement was the book of 2 Timothy, which you are about to study. Think of it as a dying man's last word, inspired by the Holy Spirit of God.

Second Timothy teaches faithfulness to God. In our first study of chapter 1 we see two faithful servants of the Lord, Paul and Timothy.

Paul, a Faithful Servant

Paul was again in prison as he wrote 2 Timothy. Let's briefly review the history of Paul as he wrote Philemon, Titus and 2 Timothy.

Paul had been in prison as he wrote Philemon. That imprisonment seems to have been the one found in Acts 28. At the end of Paul's three missionary journeys he was taken into custody in Palestine and held for over two years. Finally he appealed to Caesar and made the trip to Rome to present his case before Caesar.

He arrived in Rome and was permitted to dwell in his own place, but with a soldier to guard him. This has been described as a house arrest. Even in his house arrest he was chained to prevent his escaping. Paul was able to receive visitors. He ministered to saints who came to visit him, as well as presented the gospel to the soldiers who were sent to guard him. He even evangelized some outsiders, such as Philemon.

After two years of house arrest Paul apparently received a hearing before Caesar and was set free. A number of references to his journeys in some of the New Testament epistles do not seem to fit into the three missionary journeys as described in the book of Acts.

No clear itinerary of Paul's travels after he was released is given, but it appears that he went to Crete (Titus 1:5), to Ephesus (1 Tim. 1:3; 3:14), possibly to Colosse where he had wanted to visit Philemon (Philemon 22), to Macedonia (1 Tim. 1:3), perhaps to Philippi (Phil. 2:24), to Nicopolis (Titus 3:12), to Miletus (2 Tim. 4:20), to Troas (2 Tim. 4:13), to Corinth (2 Tim. 4:20), perhaps even to Spain as he had desired (Rom. 15:24) and finally back to imprisonment in Rome (2 Tim. 1:16, 17).

Paul had written to Philemon while under house arrest in Rome. He had written to Titus during the time of release. Finally he wrote 2 Timothy during his second imprisonment.

There is no doubt that Paul was in jail as he wrote the epistle of 2 Timothy. He spoke of himself as the prisoner of the Lord (1:8) and of his chains (1:16). He asked Timothy to come to him, bringing certain things, including his cloak (4:9-13). Perhaps he was in that well-known prison which was a cold, dark, damp place. And he desired that Timothy might bring his coat for warmth and comfort when winter hit the prison.

This prison where Paul was held must have been in Rome, for he mentioned that when Onesiphorus had been in Rome he sought very diligently to find Paul (2 Tim. 1:17). Paul's whereabouts during this imprisonment were not well-known, and Onesiphorus had to search and go through bureaucratic red tape to discover Paul's location. But he did manage to do it.

When Paul wrote to Timothy from a Roman prison, he had already had one hearing at which he had the opportunity to present the gospel (4:16, 17). He was in prison for preaching the gospel and so it was very relevant to his defense to explain that gospel. It provided a unique opportunity for him to present Jesus Christ to the entire court.

At his first defense no human stood with him (4:16). How tragic! But God stood with him, and God strengthened him so that he could present a bold and clear testimony for Jesus Christ (4:17).

He was awaiting his second hearing as he wrote to Timothy. We might call that hearing the declaration of judgment or the passing of sentence. The trial was over and Paul was waiting for the decision to come down. He had been vindicated when he was imprisoned the first time, just as he had expected. Remember, he asked Philemon to prepare lodging for him, for he trusted to be released and to visit Colosse (Philemon 22).

But as he wrote to Timothy from his second imprisonment he was not optimistic at all. In fact he anticipated death (2 Tim. 4:6–8). He expected that he would soon be martyred for Jesus Christ, and so he wrote 2 Timothy, expecting to die. History indicates that his expectations were realized.

Timothy, a Faithful Servant

Paul addressed his final letter to Timothy. Who

was this man? His father was a Greek and his mother was Jewish (Acts 16:1). His mother and grandmother had been believers in the God of the Bible (2 Tim. 1:5). Timothy himself had known the Old Testament Scriptures from his childhood days (2 Tim. 3:15).

Apparently Timothy came to know Jesus Christ through Paul's preaching on his first missionary journey. Paul called Timothy his son in the faith (1 Tim. 1:2).

When Paul returned to the area of Derbe and Lystra (Timothy's home) on his second missionary journey, Timothy was well reported of by the brethren. He had a good reputation as one who was growing in the grace and knowledge of Jesus Christ. So Paul selected Timothy to join the missionary team and continue with Paul in spreading the gospel (Acts 16:3).

Timothy traveled with Paul through most of that second missionary journey and the third journey. A deep relationship developed between the two men. In 2 Timothy Paul referred to Timothy as his dearly beloved son (1:2). Strong bonds of love had developed over the years. Paul also referred to Timothy as his brother, a minister of God, and a fellow laborer in the gospel of Christ (1 Thess. 3:2).

Paul made the astounding statement that he had no man like-minded with himself as was Timothy. And he proceeded to say that Timothy had served with him in the gospel ministry as a son serving a father (Phil. 2:2, 22). Through their missionary journeys together Paul and Timothy became true fellow workers (Rom. 16:21).

Paul also sent Timothy on various missions. Paul sent him to Corinth to remind the Corinthians of Paul's ways, which were the ways of

Christ, and to remind them of how Paul had taught them and demonstrated to them the message and life that Christ offered (1 Cor. 4:17).

Timothy was also sent to Thessalonica. When Paul had been personally present in Thessalonica, he warned the people of afflictions, suffering and tribulation to come. And after he had left the town, he knew the Thessalonian believers were going through those hard times, so he sent Timothy to establish them and comfort them concerning their faith in Christ as they faced opposition. Timothy then traveled back to be with Paul and was a bearer of good news, letting Paul know how the Thessalonians were standing true to God (1 Thess. 3:1-6).

Timothy was with Paul as the apostle drew his third missionary journey to a close and headed toward Jerusalem (Acts 20:1-4). And Timothy was with Paul in Rome during Paul's first Roman imprisonment (Philemon 1), for Paul wrote from that imprisonment and included Timothy in his introductory greetings.

After Paul was freed from that first jailing and was making some of his evangelistic trips, he placed Timothy in Ephesus (1 Tim. 1:3) and asked him to stay there for a while to do some very important things for the church there.

False teachers had entered, even as Paul had predicted when he met with the Ephesian elders (Acts 20:17, 28-31). Timothy was commissioned to combat that false doctrine. He was given the responsibility to impart to the church God's standards of church leadership and to ordain the elders that met the standard.

When Paul was returned to Rome for his final imprisonment, Timothy was still in Ephesus. Paul wrote 2 Timothy to him, urging him to be faithful to the Lord and to sound doctrine. Paul was passing from the scene, and if anything was on his heart it was the need for *faithfulness* in the people of God and in the leadership who direct the people of God. His second letter to Timothy would focus upon the important quality of faithfulness.

The Bible encourages hearts by showing that even the great men of faith were human, men of passions like yours and mine. Timothy was a great worker in the gospel and a companion of Paul, and yet he faced struggles in his life.

He faced the struggle of youthfulness. Paul instructed him to let no man despise his youth, but to be an example to the believers (1 Tim. 4:12). And he was told to flee youthful lusts (2 Tim. 2:22).

Putting the chronology together, Timothy had been a believer for about fifteen years by this time, so he was no novice in the faith. He probably was in his thirties, but he lacked the hoary head that would command the respect of old age.

Timothy also faced the struggle of physical problems. He had a chronic or recurrent stomach problem, and Paul instructed him to follow the common medicinal practice of that day and take a little wine for the sake of his stomach (1 Tim. 5:23). Perhaps his nature and personality were such that the pressures of the ministry gave him indigestion or even an ulcer.

Finally, he may have faced the struggle of timidity, for Paul instructed him that he should not be ashamed of the testimony of the Lord nor of Paul, who was in prison (2 Tim. 1:8). It may be that Timothy did not have some of the boldness that Paul could demonstrate in his ministry for Christ.

Timothy faced his struggles, just as you and I, and yet he was a beloved fellow worker in the gospel, well respected, greatly trusted, and quite effective in furthering the work of the Lord Jesus Christ.

8 Faithfulness in History

Verse to Memorize

2 Timothy 2:2—"And the things that thou hast heard of me among many witnesses, the same commit thou to faithful men, who shall be able to teach others also."

Daily Bible Readings

Monday—Gospel and Grace—
   1 Corinthians 15:1-10
Tuesday—Not of Works;
   unto Works—Ephesians 2:1-10
Wednesday—An Eternal Weight of Glory—
   2 Corinthians 4:17—5:11
Thursday—Suffering for Christ—Philippians
   1:21-29
Friday—Running into Trouble—Hebrews
   11:32—12:2
Saturday—More Precious than Gold—
   1 Peter 1:1-11
Sunday—Beginning with Us—1 Peter 4:12—5:1

Search and Ponder

1. Who saw the risen Christ (1 Cor. 15:4-8)? _____

2. The saved person has been "created in Christ Jesus unto _____

_____" (Eph. 2:10).

3. In what two ways did persecuted Paul describe the afflictions which Christians suffer (2 Cor. 4:17)? _____

_____

_____

4. In what two ways did Paul describe the future glory which awaits the Christian (2 Cor. 4:17)? _____

_____

5. What happens to the Christian when he dies; that is, when his spirit leaves his body (2 Cor. 5:8; Phil. 1:23)? _____

_____

6. Two things were given to the Philippians on behalf of Christ? _____-

_____ and _____

_____ (Phil. 1:29).

7. How were the heroes of faith in Hebrews 11:32-35 different from the heroes of faith in verses 35-38? _____

_____

How were they all the same? _____

_____

8. Describe the inheritance which belongs to every believer (1 Pet. 1:4). _____

_____

9. What could be more precious than gold (1 Pet. 1:7)? _____

10. God has saved us and called us, not according to our works, but according to _____

_____

(2 Tim. 1:9).

**Bible
Portion
to Read**   2 Timothy 1:8—2:2

Henry Stuphen, an eloquent and godly preacher, was rudely dragged from sleep and forced to walk barefoot to the place of his execution. While flames leaped about his body, the tormentors heaped insults upon him and even slashed him with knives. Such were the persecutions of Charles V against German Reformation pastors who dared to stand upon the Scriptures only and refuse to add manmade requirements to the gospel of Christ.

This chapter in our study focuses on faithfulness to God even in the face of suffering. We in the United States know very little of suffering for Jesus, at least in the sense of property confiscation, torture and death.

Throughout history those who stood for God have often been persecuted. Old Testament believers endured all sorts of torture (Heb. 11:32—12:2). New Testament saints likewise faced the wrath of hostile governments and other power structures. The book of Acts records various persecutions and even martyrdom. The apostle

Paul summarized the type of suffering he had to endure in his second letter to the church at Corinth (2 Cor. 11:23–33).

God expects His children to remain true to Him even when such faithfulness threatens their well-being. The wonderful blessing is that He provides the enabling to do so. Second Timothy presents examples of faithfulness, as well as unfaithfulness. It also reveals the way in which Paul could remain faithful to God while being persecuted.

God's Faithfulness

Faithfulness in its perfect form resides in God. Moses declared God's faithfulness when he exhorted Israel to "know therefore that the LORD thy God, he is God, the faithful God, who keepeth covenant and mercy with them [who] love him and keep his commandments to a thousand generations" (Deut. 7:9).

The Thessalonians' encouragement came from the fact that "faithful is he that calleth you, who also will do it" (1 Thess. 5:24). The great hymn "Great Is Thy Faithfulness" heralds a blessed truth.

David told the Lord that he had declared His faithfulness and His salvation (Ps. 40:10). Faithfulness and salvation were in Paul's thoughts as he wrote of God's faithfulness in salvation

Paul said that the basis of God's saving and calling was His own purpose and grace (2 Tim. 1:9). God's purpose to save was established before the world began. Before the creation of the world (Gen. 1; 2), before the successive ages of time, God decided to provide salvation for the humans He planned to create and who He knew would fall into sin.

The Bible looks back to eternity past when it says that God chose us in Him before the foundation of the world (Eph. 1:4). The same boundless past is in view when it says that the substitutionary death of Christ, the sacrificial Lamb of God, was foreordained before the foundation of the world (1 Pet. 1:18-20). The saving death of Christ was purposed by God before creation according to Revelation 13:8 and 17:8. God established some very ambitious purposes before He even created the stage of the world upon which those purposes would be enacted.

But Paul proceeded to show that God faithfully carries out His purposes. The purpose and grace of God, established before the world was begun, have been somewhat hidden down through the ages. That is not to say they have been absolutely hidden. The Old Testament revealed many of God's purposes and much of His grace.

Yet it was only in the actual arrival of Christ and in His death on the cross that the saving purposes of God and His grace were so fully made known or manifest (2 Tim. 1:10). John informed first century Christians that the law was given by Moses, but that grace and truth came by Jesus Christ (John 1:16, 17).

When Jesus Christ came, He bore our sins in His own body on the tree, graciously paying our debt of sin, so that God might be both just and the Justifier of those who come to Him by faith in Christ (1 Pet. 2:24). Jesus Christ provided that salvation, which had been planned before the world was founded.

God made great plans before the foundation of the world, and then He carried them out according to the full extent planned in the work of Christ at His first coming. God demonstrated His attribute of faithfulness by faithfully carrying through on His ancient purposes. God *is* faithful.

Paul's Faithfulness

Paul, following the character of the Lord, remained faithful and set an example of faithfulness for us as stewards of the grace of God. Paul had been appointed a preacher, an apostle and a teacher of the gospel. The honored position earned Paul opposition. He suffered beatings, stoning, many perils, verbal abuse, weariness, hunger and thirst, exposure to the elements and imprisonment. As he wrote to Timothy he sat on death row awaiting execution. All of these things came to Paul because of his identification with Jesus Christ, not because of his own wrongdoing.

However, Paul remained faithful to his calling. He did not shrink back in cowardice or shame from standing true to his Lord. What kept him faithful through such extreme difficulties?

Paul revealed to Timothy the source of the boldness which kept him going on for God. He knew whom he had believed (2 Tim. 1:12). Paul knew his Savior, his Lord, his God. Knowing God had been Paul's great desire (Phil. 3:10). The knowledge that comes from experience and is gained by a daily walk with Christ created firm convictions in Paul. Those convictions were that Jehovah is really God, that the gospel is really true and that it is worth continuing on God's side even though the heat gets intense. Paul knew whom he had believed.

Not only did Paul know God by experience, but he was persuaded that God could keep or preserve him (2 Tim. 1:12). Paul had committed himself to God. Those who suffer according to the will of God (not for their own sins) should commit the keeping of their souls to God, as unto a faithful Creator (1 Pet. 4:19). This Paul had done. And he believed that God would keep his soul safe all the way to the Judgment Seat of Christ. Therefore, he had nothing to fear from persecution. Even though the enemies of the gospel might take his life, his soul would remain unscathed.

Paul was faithful to God and to God's purposes for him. Opposition could not deter him from faithfulness, for he knew God and he had committed himself to God's faithful care.

Onesiphorus' Faithfulness

Onesiphorus had been faithful to Paul, the Lord's servant, both at Ephesus and at Rome (2 Tim. 1:16–18). When Paul ministered in Ephesus, Onesiphorus had ministered to him in some unspecified way. After Paul was imprisoned in Rome, this man diligently searched to locate the apostle. When he found him, he ministered to Paul. Paul was refreshed by Onesiphorus.

Onesiphorus' faithfulness in the face of difficulties became another example to Timothy, and to us.

Unfaithful Ones

Not everyone is faithful. Only God is faithful in the absolute sense. Paul and Onesiphorus had been, but others had not. Timothy knew by personal experience that all they "who are in Asia" had turned away from Paul (2 Tim. 1:15).

Paul said that at his first hearing or trial no man stood with him, but all forsook him (2 Tim. 4:16). Probably some people from Asia had been in Rome with Paul at the time of his trial, and they had all forsaken him. As Paul wrote, those people from Asia had returned to Asia, and so Paul referred to them as all who "are" in Asia.

Unfaithfulness is a very real and present danger. The Asians, including Phygellus and Hermogenes, set a tragic example.

Timothy Charged to Faithfulness

The examples of faithfulness on the part of God and Paul and of unfaithfulness on the part of the Asians form the setting in which Timothy was charged to be faithful (2 Tim. 1:13; 2:1, 2). Timothy was to be faithful in three areas: doctrine, grace and reproduction.

Sound doctrine (healthful, health-producing doctrine) is very important. It brings about spiritual life and health because it comes from God Himself. Timothy was to hold such doctrine fast. He must see the importance of correct doctrine and faithfully cling to it as a drowning man would cling to a life preserver.

Holding on to sound doctrine is vitally important. But the manner in which one holds faithfully to orthodoxy is also important. The correct manner for holding fast sound words is in faith and love. Timothy must genuinely believe sound doctrine with all his heart, mind and soul. And he must hold sound doctrine with a caring concern, with love for God and for his neighbor. Cold, dead orthodoxy falls short of God's desire.

> Holding on to sound doctrine is vitally important. But the manner in which one holds faithfully to orthodoxy is also important. . . . Our orthodoxy must be alive with a living faith and with a heartwarming love.

Our orthodoxy must be alive with a living faith and with a heartwarming love.

Timothy was to be faithful in God's grace (2:1). "Grace" here speaks of the blessings which God's attribute of grace provides for the Christian. Timothy should be strong in the power, the love and the sound mind provided by God (1:7). It is all too easy to neglect God's gracious provisions for us, so faithfulness in laying hold of them is our challenge.

Timothy was to be faithful in reproduction as well (2:2). Paul knew he would soon be taken in death. He was concerned about the preservation or continuation of sound doctrine. So he instructed Timothy to pass it on to others who possessed two qualities: faithfulness and the ability to teach others. As Timothy was faithful in all these things, Christian truth continued to flourish.

The examples of faithfulness and the danger of unfaithfulness face us today. They both make the command to be faithful an urgent exhortation to us.

9 Faithfulness Illustrated

Verse to Memorize

2 Timothy 2:10—"Therefore I endure all things for the elect's sakes, that they may also obtain the salvation which is in Christ Jesus with eternal glory."

Daily Bible Readings

Monday—A Risen Lord—1 Corinthians 15:20-28

Tuesday—Time to Choose—Joshua 24:14-25

Wednesday—The Christian Soldier—Ephesians 6:11-20

Thursday—Following Jesus—John 15:18-27

Friday—Marks of Ministry—2 Corinthians 11:23-33

Saturday—For the Gospel's Sake—1 Corinthians 9:19-27

Sunday—God's Faithfulness—Psalm 89:1-8

Search and Ponder

1. The last enemy which Christ will destroy is ——————— (1 Cor. 15:26).

2. Joshua challenged the people

to choose whether they would serve God or something else (Josh. 24:15). What decision have you made personally about serving God? _____

_____

3. The armor of God is the Christian's defense against Satan and demons. The seven elements of the armor, listed in Ephesians 6:13–17, are _____

_____

_____ .

4. According to John 15:26, Jesus Christ taught that when the Holy Spirit should come, He would _____ .

5. John 15:23 tells us that if a person hates Jesus, then he _____ .

6. What can a Christian expect, according to John 15:20? _____

_____

7. When false teachers sought to discredit the Lord's apostle, Paul demonstrated his genuineness by a list of credentials (2 Cor. 11:23–27). How would you summarize these credentials? _____

_____

8. Paul was all things to all men, that he might by all means save some (1 Cor. 9:22). How could you apply this principle to be a more effective witness to someone you know? _____

_____

_____

9. What motivated Paul to endure persecution for preaching the gospel (2 Tim. 2:10)? _____

_____

10. What can God not do, according to 2 Timothy 2:13? _____

Bible Portion to Read   2 Timothy 2:3–13

The German army of the World War II era developed incredible discipline. It has been said that the discipline was so strict that many a soldier would have taken his own life if ordered to do so.

The Christian serves as a soldier under the perfect Commanding Officer. God is the only all-wise Commander, and His heart overflows with caring concern and tender affection for His troops. Certainly Christians should obey and be faithful to Him.

The Soldier

The illustration of a soldier is the first of several illustrations of Christian faithfulness given in 2 Timothy 2:3–13. The soldier teaches us to endure hardness (v. 3). Life in the combat zone is rough. Sleep is short; food is plain; the work is strenuous; the pressure is fatiguing, and the risk of impending death hangs over everything. But the faithful soldier endures. He does not go AWOL or shoot himself in the foot.

The soldier also teaches us to have a singleness of purpose (v. 4). The Roman soldier of Paul's day, more than many a modern soldier, cut himself off from the affairs of everyday life and gave himself wholeheartedly to soldiering.

Civilian life-style ended. His purpose for the duration of his tour of duty was only to please the one who had chosen him to be a soldier.

The Christian is presented as a soldier of Christ several times in the New Testament. As His soldiers, we should have His service as our single purpose. Our tour of duty ends with our death. We have needs of this life for which to care, but those needs can be satisfied in a way that would please the One Who has chosen us to be His soldier.

When combat with evil forces gets intense, and when the flesh and blood, through which the evil forces often work, attack from all directions at once, we as Christian soldiers must endure. We must neither surrender to them nor desert our post.

The Athlete

The second illustration of faithfulness is an athlete (v. 5). The athlete teaches us to follow the rules and regulations. The Olympic runner of Paul's day was disqualified from winning if he broke the rules. There were on-track rules concerning lanes and bumping. There were off-track rules concerning diet and other matters. To be a recognized winner an athlete had to follow those rules.

Faithfulness to God requires that we follow the commandments of Christ. We must do what He wants, and we must do it the way in which He wants it done. The end does not justify the means; only those who run lawfully receive the victor's crown at the Judgment Seat of Christ.

We Americans seem more and more enthralled with athletics, as the skyrocketing salaries of athletes indicate. Perhaps the words of John R. W. Stott would be apropos:

> The Christian life is regularly likened in the New Testament to a race, not in the sense that we are competing against each other (though we are to "outdo one another in showing honour," Rom. 12:10), but in other ways, in the strenuous self-discipline of training (1 Cor. 9:24–27), in laying aside every hindrance (Heb. 12:1, 2) and here in keeping the rules (*Guard the Gospel* [Downers Grove, IL: InterVarsity Press], p. 55).

As we think of the Christian life as a race or an athletic contest, let us focus not on competition with one another but on the three Biblical comparisons mentioned by Stott.

We would add that the Bible also commends a person's getting the reward as an athlete. In the Christian life *everyone* can win reward, not just one (2 Tim. 4:8). The idea is not to beat other believers but to exert your greatest effort so that you can receive a reward from God, just as a winning runner receives a reward from the judge (1 Cor. 9:24).

The Farmer

Paul's third illustration of faithfulness is that of a farmer (2 Tim. 2:6). The farmer teaches us to labor, to work to the point of exhaustion, pain or fatigue. Farm work today demands great physical stamina. Think of what it demanded when most everything had to be done by hand and the most advanced equipment was an ox-drawn plow. Faithfulness to God demands spiritual stamina that can do good and not grow weary in well-doing.

These three illustrations show that faithfulness involves endurance, single-minded purpose, careful obedience that keeps God's commandments, and labor. That is a challenge!

Now notice a subtheme that runs through these three illustrations. The subtheme is that faithfulness will be rewarded by God. The soldier has a single-minded purpose so that he may please him who has chosen him. The athlete strives lawfully so that he can receive a crown. The farmer who works hard is the first partaker of the fruits.

Likewise the Christian looks for a "well done thou good and faithful servant." At the Judgment Seat of Christ our deeds done in the body will be reviewed and classified as worthy of reward or unworthy of reward (1 Cor. 3:12-15; 2 Cor. 5:10). The unworthy ones will be burned by the piercing evaluation, but the worthy ones will receive wreaths of approval: "God is not unrighteous to forget your work and labour of love, which ye have [shown] toward his name . . ." (Heb. 6:10).

Paul Himself

A fourth illustration of faithfulness is Paul himself. Paul suffered trouble as an evildoer. Remember the list of suffering he recorded in 2 Corinthians 11:23-27. Paul endured all the troubles which God permitted to come his way; he did not let them turn him from faithfulness to God.

Paul showed that the faithfulness of God motivated him to be faithful to God. God was faithful in raising Christ from the dead. Jesus was born of the seed of David in fulfillment of prophecy. He suffered to the point of death, but God vindicated Him and raised Him from the dead, again as a fulfillment of prophecy. God is faithful to His Word.

Timothy, and believers today, should take heart. Even though suffering results from being faithful to God, God will be faithful to His Word to vindicate and reward the sufferer.

God is also faithful to His purposes for His Word. Paul sat in bonds as he wrote to Timothy, but the Word of God was not bound. The Word cannot be bound. Throughout history people have tried to bind, limit or destroy the Scriptures, but they never succeed.

God's Word is compared to the unfailing water cycle: "So shall my word be that goeth forth out of my mouth: it shall not return unto me void, but it shall accomplish that which I please, and it shall prosper in the thing whereto I sent it" declares the Lord Himself (Isa. 55:11). As God's faithfulness incited Paul to faithfulness, so we, too, should be moved to faithfulness in our Christian walk.

A Famous Saying

A well-known saying illustrates faithfulness. The saying Paul quoted in 2 Timothy 2:11-13 may have been a popular hymn of the early Christians, similar to "Amazing Grace" today. The saying could be counted faithful because it was accurate and true.

The saying is composed of four couplets. The first two couplets speak of faithfulness, and the last two speak of unfaithfulness.

If we reckon ourselves dead to sin and selfish desires, and if we serve God as ones who are alive unto righteousness, then we will live with Him

If we are faithful in suffering with Christ when He brings trials into our path, then we will also reign with Him when He brings us into His kingdom.

in Heaven. The Christian may not "live it up" on earth, but he can anticipate living up with God in Heaven.

If we are faithful in suffering with Christ when He brings trials into our path, then we will also reign with Him when He brings us into His kingdom. Learning to rule oneself in this life prepares one to rule others in the kingdom to come.

If we deny Him and make that the position of our lives (not just an isolated denial like Peter's by the fire), then He will deny us before His Father Who is in Heaven (v. 12; cf. Luke 12:9). If we are unfaithful, He continues faithful to His warnings and judgments, and so He will reject us in the end.

It is not possible for a genuine Christian to become lost. The Bible clearly teaches eternal security. True believers are saved forever. But the Bible also clearly teaches that there are many false professors. There are people who say they believe in Christ but who do not.

Paul warned, by use of this faithful saying, that if one makes denial of God the theme of his life, God will deny him in faithfulness to His own warnings. He cannot do otherwise, for that would be to deny Himself. This moves faithfulness out of the realm of the optional and puts it into the realm of the necessary. Faithfulness is necessary as evidence of genuine salvation.

John, the apostle of love, put it this way: "They went out from us, but they were not of us: for if they had been of us, they would no doubt have continued with us: but they went out, that they might be made manifest that they were not all of us" (1 John 2:19). The unfaithfulness of those people showed them to be false professors. Faithfulness is required of God's servants. Had they been genuine believers, they would have remained faithful.

10 Faithfulness and Life

Verse to Memorize

2 Timothy 2:19—"Nevertheless the foundation of God standeth sure, having this seal, The Lord knoweth them that are his. And, Let every one that nameth the name of Christ depart from iniquity."

Daily Bible Readings

Monday—Ignorance or Shipwreck—
   1 Timothy 1:12-20
Tuesday—God Knows His Own—
   John 10:7-18
Wednesday—A Treasure in Pottery—2 Corinthians
   4:1-10
Thursday—Blessed Vessels—Exodus 39:33-43
Friday—Flesh or Spirit—Galatians 5:16-26
Saturday—Darkness or Light—Ephesians 5:1-11
Sunday—Delivered from Captivity—Ezra 6:16-22

Search and Ponder

1. Is it possible for a blasphemer to become a minister (1 Tim. 1:12, 13)?

_____

2. What does Satan do to keep lost

people from being saved (2 Cor. 4:4)? _____

_____

3. How is the evil work of Satan overcome (2 Cor. 4:6)? _____

_____

4. When all the tabernacle components were completed and inspected, what was Moses' evaluation of the work (Exod. 39:43)? _____

_____

5. The works of the sinful flesh include things we consider terrible and things we consider not so bad. Which ones does God say are not so bad (Gal. 5:19-21)? _____

6. What could you do to cause the fruit of the Spirit to grow in your life? _____

_____

7. Imagine a little child following and imitating his parent. What can a Christian learn from such a child's behavior (Eph. 5:1)? _____

8. The Bible speaks of sins as "works of darkness." What two things should the Christian do with regard to works of darkness (Eph. 5:11)? _____

_____

9. Finish this quotation: "Let every one that nameth the name of Christ _____

_____"

(2 Tim. 2:19).

10. How should the Lord's servant handle opposition (2 Tim. 2:24-26)? _____

_____

_____

The television preacher flailed his arms at the camera, his steely eyes piercing each viewer. Anger contorted his face. Bitter hatred dripped from his words. His language was spiced with veiled profanity. As his audience watched and listened, the viewers became incensed against those of whom he was speaking. When he wished hell on his enemies, many viewers said, "Amen."

Paul instructed Timothy in the importance of sound doctrine, as well as godly behavior. He further showed that the servant of the Lord must confront those who oppose sound doctrine. But he also explained the attitude one must have as he confronts and even separates. We, too, must be Christian ladies and gentlemen. Compare the description of the TV preacher which you just read with the description of God's servant in 2 Timothy 2:24–26.

Faithfulness in Doctrine

Sound doctrine is very important to God. The word "sound" means healthful or health-producing. Sound doctrine produces spiritual health because it comes from God, the Great Physician. It is His prescription for the sickness and death of sin. Absorbing the Word of God into one's very being by meditation and faith builds robust spiritual health.

We, like Timothy, are to be workmen, who rightly divide the Word of truth (2 Tim. 2:15). "Rightly divide" means to cut a straight line. The word was used in a number of contexts in secular Greek, but Paul's primary illustration was probably its use in tentmaking, for that was his occupation. A tentmaker needed to cut things straight so they would fit together. Tents were made of animal hides, not of huge sheets of canvas or nylon such as we have today. Several animal hides had to be cut straight so that one would butt up straight against the other and they could be stitched together to make the tent.

Likewise, the workman of God is to "cut straight" through the Word of God. That is, he is to interpret it correctly, understanding its various doctrines and seeing one Scripture in the light of other Scriptures so that all fit together into one harmonious whole. In order to rightly divide the Scriptures, we must study; we must be diligent or give haste or show eagerness, even as Timothy.

Those three ideas give some good direction as to how we should study the Word of God. We ought to study it with diligence, not just when it happens to be convenient. We ought to study it with haste, not rushing through it but rushing *to* it. We ought to study God's Word with eagerness and willingness.

Every Christian should study the Word, not just church leaders and teachers. It is spiritual food to every Christian: milk for the new babes and meat for the more mature. It renews our minds, enabling us to overcome the constant defilement of the world's anti-God ideas.

We need to read the Word and meditate upon the truth of it. We should commit it to memory to cleanse our way that we might not sin against God (Ps. 119:9, 11). We need to know it so it will be at our mental fingertips as the Sword of the Spirit for battle with Satan and as the Textbook of the ages for answering those who ask a reason of the hope that is within us.

The result of diligent study of the Word is God's approval. He will examine the workman's work and declare it acceptable, or the workman will be put to shame. Would any Christian want to be put to shame when the Lord returns?

There is a danger of erring from the truth. Neglect of the Word is serious. If one's mind is filled with the eternal issues of God, then that one is unlikely to be sidetracked into error. On the other hand, if one neglects the truth of God's Word, that one becomes more susceptible to error.

Vain and profane babblings take the place of God's truth in the mind that omits diligent study of God's Word. There is a way that seems right to human reasoning and philosophy, but the ends of that way are death (Prov. 14:12).

Faithfulness in Behavior

Two godly behaviors, fleeing and following, were prescribed for Timothy (2 Tim. 2:22). Fleeing is described well in Matthew 2:13. Herod had ordered all the children of Bethlehem to be killed. An angel came to Joseph and instructed him to take the Child, Jesus, and Mary and flee to Egypt. Surely that was a flight without hesitation, done in great haste and with all the energy possible.

John the Baptist talked about fleeing from the

wrath to come (Matt. 3:7). When one fully understands the wrath of God as expressed in hell's fire, he vigorously flees to the saving arms of Jesus. As Mary and Joseph fled from the murderer of children, and as people are to flee from the wrath of God, so Christians are to flee from youthful lusts.

"Youthful lusts" would include a variety of desires that arise from the self-sufficient attitude that is characteristic of youthfulness. Any desire which springs from an attitude of independence from God is a desire we should flee from.

The "following after" is also to be with intensity. It is a chasing after. Paul confessed that he had persecuted the Church of God and wasted it (Gal. 1:13). He pursued Christians, chasing them all the way from Jerusalem to Damascus, to lay hold of them.

The Christian must follow after righteousness, faith, love and peace with the same tenacity (2 Tim. 2:22). "Righteousness" speaks of right conduct before God and is the total opposite of youthful desires.

God knows them that are His. He knows who is really saved. Some who make a profession of faith in Christ do it insincerely, but the Lord sees the thoughts and intents of the heart. He knows His sheep. Christ also taught that His sheep hear His voice and follow Him.

"Let every one that nameth the name of Christ depart from iniquity" (2 Tim. 2:19), Paul instructed. This verse reminds us of the necessity of godly behavior. Those who name Christ's name are those who call upon the Lord for salvation, who name Him as Lord and Savior (Rom. 10:13). Every such person is to depart from iniquity.

Christians are to be separated from sinful practices and from so-called brothers who stubbornly continue in sinful practices. Separation from such makes one a vessel fit for God's use, prepared unto every good work, sanctified and honorable (2 Tim. 2:21).

Faithfulness in Controversy

Timothy was commanded to avoid foolish and unlearned questions (v. 23). These questions would be speculations beyond the Word of God, like the words to no profit (v. 14), profane and vain babbling (v. 16) and words that eat like gangrene (v. 17).

Is the Christian to avoid all controversy? Other passages teach that there is a proper place for pointing out error and defending the truth. Verses 24 through 26 in this context state that the servant of the Lord must proclaim truth and correct those who teach error. Jude urged believers to contend earnestly for the faith (Jude 3). Paul charged the Ephesian elders to protect the flock of God against false teaching. Such actions risk controversy, for those in error seldom submit easily to the truth.

There is an important place for showing that a particular doctrine is unscriptural. But there also comes a time when the error has been so clearly exposed by Scripture that further explanations would be pointless. The Bible student argues his point and knows when to rest his case.

Also, there are times when speculative teaching is proclaimed which does not find its base clearly in Scripture and which cannot clearly be refuted from Scripture. We must be careful to adhere to what the Bible says and not get drawn away into speculations that are beyond the Word of God. This seems to be a temptation to fundamental Christians in the unrevealed details of prophecy. The Lord's children need to be careful about getting into controversy over speculative areas.

The message of 2 Timothy 2:23 is not to avoid confronting foolish and unlearned questions but to avoid getting involved in them. God gives us the method, the manner and the purpose in dealing with such issues.

The method of dealing with them is instruction (v. 25). The servant of the Lord must instruct opposers. Opposers raise unlearned questions, and God's servant gives instruction which will properly deal with those questions. God's servant stands up to the babbler and points out where his babblings are wrong according to the Word of God, which the servant has rightly divided.

The manner of instructing opposers is important. The Lord's servant must not get involved in producing strife, but be gentle to all, able to teach and patient (v. 24). As he clearly and accurately presents the truth and is opposed, he must not become personally insulted. It is not his truth or honor that is at stake, but God's. The servant realizes that only by God's grace has he come to understand and value God's truth, and so he instructs the babbler with an attitude of meekness.

The ultimate purpose in instructing babblers is not to embarrass them nor even to merely prove them wrong. The goal is that they might come to know the truth (vv. 25, 26). It is the love of the truth of God that drives God's servant to study and defend the Bible. And God's servant desires that the babbler might come to view the truth with the same love.

Learning spiritual truth involves more than mere human teaching. The unsaved person does not understand spiritual truth (1 Cor. 2:14). The Holy Spirit must teach the babbler; he will acknowledge the truth only if God gives him repentance. The Lord's servant instructs with gentleness, meekness and patience, trusting God to work as He sovereignly will.

Babblers have been intoxicated and snared by the devil. The Evil One has caught them with godless philosophy. He has taken them captive at his will, and they need to "recover themselves," which literally means that they need to become sober again.

To be faithful to God in controversy is to stand firmly for the truth. But it is to stand with the proper attitudes and manner and for the right purpose. And it is to do all this with a sense of dependence upon God, realizing that He is the One, ultimately, Who must give repentance.

11 Faithfulness and Apostasy

Verse to Memorize

2 Timothy 3:14—"But continue thou in the things which thou hast learned and hast been assured of, knowing of whom thou hast learned them."

Daily Bible Readings

Monday—The Last Days—1 John 2:18-29

Tuesday—Biblical Creeps—Jude 3-13

Wednesday—Creeps and Christians—Jude 14-25

Thursday—Temporary Success—Exodus 7:8-13, 19-22; 8:5-7, 16-19

Friday—Afflictions in Asia—Acts 13:50-52; 14:1-7, 19-22

Saturday—Be Sober—1 Thessalonians 5:1-11

Sunday—Spirit-moved—2 Peter 1:15-21

Search and Ponder

1. What time was it when John wrote 1 John 2:18? _____

2. First John 2:23 tells us that if a person denies Jesus is the Christ, then

he _____ .

3. Michael, the archangel, dared not bring a railing accusation against the devil, but said, "The Lord rebuke thee" (Jude 9). How would you apply that to the way we speak to and about the devil? __

_____

4. Who is our Savior, according to Jude 25? __

_____

5. The magicians of Egypt were able to imitate three of God's miracles through Moses. When they could not imitate the fourth miracle, what did they conclude (Exod. 8:19)? _____

_____

6. A person must be born again to enter the kingdom of God. Acts 14:22 tells us that the road by which the born-again ones travel to the kingdom leads through _____

_____ .

7. God has made an appointment for each Christian. That appointment is not to _____-_____ but to _____-_____ (1 Thess. 5:9).

8. Men of God proclaimed the Word of God as they _____

_____ (2 Pet. 1:21).

9. All that will live godly in Christ Jesus shall _____ (2 Tim. 3:12).

10. Second Timothy 3:16 declares that all Scripture is profitable for _____

_____ .

Remember Dr. Jekyll? People respected him as a renowned medical man, but he had another side, the evil Mr. Hyde. "All that glitters is not gold" goes the saying, and all who have a form of godliness are not followers of God.

False religion condemns the soul of its adherents, and brings danger and difficulty to true Christians. Second Timothy 3 speaks pointedly of the perilous times created by false religion in the last days.

The Character and Deeds of Reprobates

False religion has been true Christianity's greatest persecutor. The last days are perilous times because reprobate religionists arise who are a peril to true believers. In his letter to Timothy Paul presented nineteen characteristics of these reprobates; one thread seems to run through all the characteristics. The basic problem with these people relates to their love.

The very first quality is that they shall be lovers of their own selves, and the last quality is that they shall be lovers of pleasure more than lovers of God. The second quality is translated "covetous" and literally means lovers of silver or money. Furthermore, these people are without natural affection. They are "despisers of those who are good" or literally, not lovers of good. Four of the nineteen qualities deal with love, and one deals with affection.

Our culture craves love. It seems to have a fixation on love, and yet love eludes it. Sin has corrupted every part of the human being, including his affections. A society apart from God has problems with love.

Reprobates resist the truth as Jannes and Jambres withstood Moses (2 Tim. 3:8). Pharaoh was able to get some magicians of Egypt who could duplicate, or appear to duplicate, miracles of Moses. They threw down their rods and made them become serpents (Exod. 7:11). They used their enchantments to turn water into blood (Exod. 7:22). They sought to reproduce what Moses was doing, and thus they withstood his message. Scripture doesn't say specifically how they did this, whether by sleight of hand or by satanic power.

The reprobates of the last days resist the truth in a similar manner. Some see the comparison as merely that both Moses' opponents and modern-day teachers resist the message of God. Some would go farther and say that as Jannes and Jambres resisted the truth by using magical arts, so the producers of perilous times would use magical arts. That may well be true.

In the church at Ephesus there were people who had been involved in magical arts before they came to know Christ. You will remember that when Paul's ministry in Ephesus was successful, many people who had used curious or magical arts previous to their conversion brought their books together and burned them (Acts 19:19). Timothy was serving in Ephesus as he received this letter. It would not be at all surprising to learn that those in Ephesus who had a form of godliness but denied the power thereof were using magical arts to duplicate the miracles that Paul had performed there (Acts 19:11, 12) in order to get followers.

Also, remember that in the coming Tribulation, when the man of sin is revealed, he will be able to do magical things. He will have all power, signs and lying wonders. These workings will be according to the working of Satan. Satanic power can do miraculous things. The ability to perform a miracle is not a guarantee that the person is from God.

The Comprehension of Timothy

Others may turn away from God, but Timothy must continue faithful (2 Tim. 3:14ff.). He must be faithful to Paul's example, which he knew so well. Paul exhorted the Corinthians to be followers of him even as he was of Christ (1 Cor. 11:1). He wanted the Philippians to follow him and to mark with special attention those who walked as he walked (Phil. 3:17).

Timothy was to follow Paul's doctrine. Paul had received it from God (Gal. 1:1ff.), so it was sound doctrine which expressed God's will. Timothy was to follow Paul's manner of life, which conformed to the moral commands of Jesus Christ. He was to follow Paul's purpose. Paul summarized his purpose as telling both Jews and Gentiles that they should repent and do works suitable to repentance (Acts 26:19, 20).

Timothy was to follow Paul's faith. Paul trusted God and was faithful to God. Timothy was to follow Paul in his long-suffering with people who rejected and reviled him, in his love for God and others, in his patience with difficult circumstances and in his persecutions and afflictions. Paul specifically mentioned the troubles he had at three cities, for they were Timothy's hometown area, and they were the places where the most extreme persecution took place (Acts 14:19-21).

God delivered Paul out of all those things. Similarly, Christ was delivered from those who sought His harm many times because it was not yet time for Him to die. Christ and Paul were invincible until their work was done. Likewise, as we walk faithfully with God, you and I will live until we have accomplished His purpose for us.

Paul and Christ suffered; Timothy suffered; "Yea, and all that will live godly in Christ Jesus shall suffer persecution" (2 Tim. 3:12). Christ said that the world hates Christians as it hated Him first, and the servant is no greater than his master (John 15:18-20). He said His followers would have tribulation in the world, but to be of good cheer for He had overcome the world (John 16:33).

Paul encouraged suffering Christians with the message that Christians, through much tribulation, enter into the kingdom of God (Acts 14:22). He wrote to the Thessalonians who suffered persecution that no man should be moved by afflictions, for Christians are appointed to such things (1 Thess. 3:3).

How much do you and I suffer for Christ? The early Christians suffered while they were in the world seeking to minister to the world and because they were different from the world. Often we lack opposition because we are not different enough from the world for the world to notice, or because we are not in contact with the world so they can notice the difference.

All that will live *godly* shall suffer persecution. It may not be official persecution from the government in a land like ours where there is religious liberty. It may come from individuals who are upset by our stand.

All that "will" live godly means all who desire to live godly, who make godliness their purpose. Vain babblings increase unto more ungodliness, but the followers of God have a desire to live godly and to work that desire out in their daily lives.

Timothy knew Paul's teaching and Paul's example. He knew it by personally traveling with Paul and witnessing Paul's life. As evil men and seducers grew worse and worse, Timothy must fall back on the example of godliness which he found in Paul.

The Continuance of Timothy

Timothy must "continue" or stand firm (2 Tim. 3:14). This word is translated "abide" in John 15, where we are told to abide in Christ. Christians are to be growing in certain areas, but there are also areas in which we are to maintain our position. Timothy was to abide in the doctrine he had learned. He could learn additional doctrine, but he must not forsake the correct doctrine he had already been taught.

He was to continue in the doctrine he had learned because he had been assured it was correct and because of who taught it to him. Paul, the apostle of Jesus Christ, was his teacher. He was to continue in the doctrine because it agreed with the Old Testament, which he had known from a child through his mother and grandmother.

Paul testified to Agrippa that his message contained no other things "than those which the prophets and Moses did say should come: That Christ should suffer, that he should be the first that should rise from the dead, and should shew light unto the people, and to the Gentiles" (Acts 26:22, 23).

Paul preached from the Old Testament, especially when speaking to Jews (Acts 17:2). The Bereans searched their Old Testaments to see if the things Paul taught were so (Acts 17:10–12). The Old Testament Scriptures were able to make one wise unto salvation because they foretold Christ's coming, dying for sin, and rising again.

Timothy had known these Scriptures since childhood. The Scriptures held the doctrine in which Timothy should abide. These Scriptures have God as their origin. They are inspired of God, or God-breathed.

As you speak, you breathe out. Try to say something while holding your breath. You cannot do it. In 2 Timothy 3:16 God is pictured as breathing out as He spoke, so that His breath forms His words. All Scripture (writing) is God-breathed. All is the very Word of God. And since all comes from God, it is all holy.

These Scriptures from God are useful or "profitable" in four areas. They are profitable for doctrine, teaching us what we should believe. They are profitable for reproof, pointing out what is wrong in both belief and behavior. They are profitable for correction, showing what is right and should be substituted for the wrong. And they are profitable for child-training in righteous living, which may summarize what has been said. If the profitableness of Scripture grips us, we will have no trouble finding time to spend in it.

The goal of Scripture's profitableness is that the man of God (the person of God, not limited to males) may be perfect, throughly furnished

> As a fundamental, Bible-believing Christian, don't limit the Scripture to just doctrine. It is our only rule of faith, yes, but also it's our rule of practice. We need to be *doing* what we are professing to believe.

unto all good works. The word "perfect" means complete, equipped, fitted out just right. The word translated "throughly furnished" is from the same root as "perfect." Perhaps Paul was thinking of the Christian soldier with his whole armor, his weapons and his shield. A soldier could be effective only when completely outfitted. Or perhaps he was thinking of the workman who needs to have all the proper tools.

The Scripture completely furnishes us for every good work. It comes from God and makes us useful to God. As a fundamental, Bible-believing Christian, don't limit the Scripture to just doctrine. It is our only rule of faith, yes, but also it's our rule of practice. We need to be *doing* what we are professing to believe.

12 Faithfulness in Ministry

Verse to Memorize 2 Timothy 4:7, 8—"I have fought a good fight, I have finished my course, I have kept the faith: Henceforth there is laid up for me a crown of righteousness, which the Lord, the righteous judge, shall give me at that day: and not to me only, but unto all them also that love his appearing."

Daily Bible Readings

Monday—God the Judge—Psalm 96:1-3

Tuesday—Father and Son Are One—John 10:22-33

Wednesday—Ready to Die—John 17:1-10

Thursday—Kept as One—John 17:11-24

Friday—Evangelizing—2 Corinthians 5:18—6:10

Saturday—Casting Crowns—Revelation 4

Sunday—His Appearing—1 Thessalonians 4:9-18

Search and Ponder

1. Why did the Jews want to stone Jesus to death (John 10:30-33)? _____

_____

2. What could cause one of Jesus' sheep (Christians) to lose eternal life and perish (John 10:27-30)? _____

3. To whom has the Son been given power (authority) to give eternal life (John 17:2)? _____

_____

4. What people did the Son ask the Father to keep (guard, protect) through His name (John 17:11)? _____

5. God created all things for _____-_____ (Rev. 4:11).

6. God was teaching the Thessalonian Christians to love each other, and they were doing it well. But what did Paul beseech them to do (1 Thess. 4:9, 10)? _____

7. How could you personally, and your Sunday School class as a group, love other Christians more? _____

_____

8. Christians who have died will come with the Lord when He comes (1 Thess. 4:14). And Christians who have died will be raised by the Lord when He comes (1 Thess. 4:16). How do these two ideas fit together? _____

_____

9. Timothy received a charge to preach what (2 Tim. 4:1, 2)? _____

10. Paul faced death knowing he had conscientiously fulfilled God's purposes for his life

(2 Tim. 4:6, 7). Are you conscientiously fulfilling God's purposes for your life? _____

**Bible
Portion
to Read**   2 Timothy 4:1-8

Deathbed conversions are thrilling, though there is room for some skepticism based on the track record of some who have made them and then lived after all. Deathbed testimonies of faithful service by longtime saints should be thrilling too. Paul gave such a testimony, and God included it in His inspired Word.

We have been studying faithfulness as taught in 2 Timothy. This chapter of our study deals with faithfulness in ministry or service for the Lord. You and I have an unspecified time left to serve our Savior. We should determine now not to count our lives dear to ourselves, but to finish the course and ministry which we have received from the Lord Jesus (Acts 20:24). Then when we reach death's door we can say with the apostle Paul, "I have fought a good fight, I have finished my course, I have kept the faith" (2 Tim. 4:7).

The Bases of Faithfulness in Ministry

Jesus Christ could come at any moment. The Bible teaches Christians to be waiting and watching for the Lord's return. Paul sometimes spoke as though he would be alive when Christ came. At other times he spoke as though he would die before Christ came. Paul's attitude reflected the fact that the Bible does not say when Christ will return. His coming is presented as imminent.

Believers down through history have had the perspective of imminency, if they have followed God's Word. Martin Luther believed that Jesus would come back in his lifetime, and we can properly believe that He may come back in ours.

When the Lord returns, He will bring with him those who have died in Christ. The graves holding their bodies will open, and their bodies, changed to be like His glorified body, will rise to meet them in the air. Then the bodies of living saints will undergo the same instantaneous transformation as they rise to meet the Lord and the departed saints (1 Thess. 4:13–18).

This message serves as a comfort to Christians bereaved over the death of spiritual brothers and sisters. But how will you and I feel if we are living when He comes? John gives us two alternatives: "And now, little children, abide in him; that, when he shall appear, we may have confidence, and not be ashamed before him at his coming" (1 John 2:28). We will feel confident, or we will be ashamed.

The possibility of shame when meeting the Lord derives from His role as Judge. Timothy was charged with ministry responsibilities "before God, and the Lord Jesus Christ, who shall judge the quick and the dead at his appearing and his kingdom" (2 Tim. 4:1)

God the Father and God the Son serve as witnesses of those charged with ministry. The idea of serving "before" God means serving in His sight. The eyes of the Lord are always upon us, and He sees the thoughts and intents of our hearts, as well as our actions. He ever sees how we are doing with the responsibilities He has entrusted to us.

He shall judge the quick (the living) and the

> The eyes of the Lord are always upon us, and He sees the thoughts and intents of our hearts, as well as our actions. He ever sees how we are doing with the responsibilities He has entrusted to us.

dead. Those who are living at His return and those who have already died will all be judged. Even if He should not come before your death or mine, He will still be our Judge to evaluate how we did with His commands to us. What a powerful incentive to faithfulness! It is no wonder that John exclaimed, "And every man that hath this hope [of Christ's return] in him purifieth himself, even as he is pure" (1 John 3:3).

Timothy had another incentive to faithfulness in addition to the judgment of God. That incentive was the appearance of those, both in the pew and in the pulpit, who could not endure sound doctrine (2 Tim. 4:3, 4). We have an abundance of such people today, and so we should also be challenged to faithfulness on this account.

There arose a sizable group of people who could not endure sound doctrine. They simply could not stand for the accurate teaching of God's holy Word. Apparently it frustrated them to have God get all the glory.

These people had ears that itched to hear things more complimentary to their fleshly pride. And so they found teachers, a "heap" of teachers, who would preach what they wanted to hear (v. 3). They turned their ears away from the truth and listened to the platitudes of the vain babblers.

You and I know that vain and profane babblings increase unto more ungodliness (2

Tim. 2:16). As these people forsook the truth for fine-sounding babbles, they were led to believe in fables.

The same phenomenon takes place around us all the time. People have ear trouble. They do not want to hear the truth. Some literally put their fingers in their ears to keep from hearing the words being spoken from God (Acts 7:57). Others do not resist so obviously, but they will not hear the truth. They manage to avoid hearing the truth by listening to teachers who do not teach it.

The Christian could be tempted to discouragement or even despair by all the closed ears he encounters. Or he could be tempted to water down the truth a little so it could receive a better hearing. But actually he should be motivated to faithfulness by the situation. God's truth must be presented. The whole counsel of God must be proclaimed with authority. After all we are God's only mouth in this world today, and God's message is the only solution to man's desperate sin problem.

The Behavior of Faithfulness in Ministry

Ministry is service. In twentieth century America the word "ministry" is often associated with the function of ordained men and considered a profession. The ministry, in the sense of pastoral service, is a noble place of service. But it is still service, and the minister is basically a servant of the Lord. Every believer is a minister-servant of Christ (John 12:26).

The New Testament instructs the servants of Christ as to the service activities God desires of them. Ministry even to one another in the Body of Christ is extensive. Christians are to admonish, forgive, comfort, edify, exhort and teach one another. They are to be at peace with each other. The most repeated command is that they love one another. On the other hand they must not judge, go to law with, bite and devour, lie to, murmur against, speak evil of nor envy one another.

God gave Timothy a list of nine behaviors which he must do as a faithful minister of Christ (2 Tim. 4:2, 5). He was to preach the Word. When we think of preaching, we think of a pastor standing behind a pulpit, giving an exposition of the Bible. But the word "preach" could be used of any authoritative proclamation of the Word. When we firmly present the message of God as "thus saith the Lord," we are proclaiming the Word authoritatively.

Timothy was to do the work of an evangelist (v. 5). The evangelist is mentioned only two other places in the New Testament, but the verb "evangelize" is used a number of times. It is usually translated "preach the gospel." An evangelist is a preacher of the gospel. Timothy was to remember the unsaved. He was not to get so immersed in caring for the flock and fighting the reprobates that he would forget the unsaved.

Finally Timothy was to make full proof of his ministry, or fulfill it completely. He was to be like Paul, who finished the course that God laid out for him to run. Timothy was to be faithful to the end.

When Paul reviewed nearly thirty years of ministry for Christ, he described it under three figures (vv. 6–8). He had fought a good fight, like a wrestler. He had finished his course, like a runner. He had kept the faith, like a soldier guarding a treasure.

The King James Version reads "*a* fight," "*my*

course" and "*the* faith." The Greek reads "*the* fight," "*the* course" and "*the* faith," reminding us that Paul viewed the whole of his life as God's plan for him (v. 7). He fought the fight God wanted him to fight. He finished the course God laid out for him. He kept the faith God revealed to him.

Paul referred to the fight as a "good fight." He did a good job fighting, but what he meant was that the fight which God had chosen for him was, by its very design in God's mind, a good fight.

Perhaps we could illustrate it like this. A person who has come up through the ranks of auto racing, beginning with midget cars, finally gets to race in the Indianapolis 500. When the race is over this rookie might say, "I ran a good race," by which he would mean he did a good job. But if he were to say, "I ran *the* good race," he would mean he had participated in the spectacular of all racing—the Indianapolis 500. Likewise, Paul had fought *the* good fight of eternal issues for God. Every Christian has the potential to be like Paul in this matter of faithfully completing the ministry God has planned for him.

Since Paul had been faithful in God's fight, on God's course and keeping God's truth, a crown of righteousness awaited him (v. 8). This crown was the leafy garland which was given to athletic winners. It had little value in itself but was held in high esteem because of the honor it signified.

There was reserved in Heaven a token of the great honor coming from no less than God Himself. The Lord, the righteous Judge, would declare that Paul had sought to live a righteous life. God would agree with Paul's evaluation of himself as recorded in verse 7.

What will God, the righteous Judge, say of you and me when we stand before His seat? Have we committed our bodies as living sacrifices to demonstrate His will in our lives? Have we made it our purpose to glorify Him in whatever we do? Are we seeking to make these commandments real in our daily lives by His grace?

All those who love Christ's appearing will receive the crown of righteousness because everyone with that hope lives righteously (v. 8).

13 Faithfulness and Paul's Companions

Verse to Memorize

2 Timothy 4:18—"And the Lord shall deliver me from every evil work, and will preserve me unto his heavenly kingdom: to whom be glory for ever and ever. Amen."

Daily Bible Readings

Monday—Love for Brothers and the World—1 John 2:7-17

Tuesday—Conflict—Acts 15:36-41

Wednesday—Resolution—Psalm 133; Colossians 4:10, 11; 2 Timothy 4:11

Thursday—Unity of the Spirit—Ephesians 3:20—4:6

Friday—Witness from Jail—Philippians 1:8-20

Saturday—Beware!—2 John 1-11

Sunday—Delivered from Evil—2 Corinthians 1:3-11

Search and Ponder

1. If we profess to be saved and hate our brother, what is our condition (1 John 2:9-11)? _____

2. What is not possible if we love

the world or the things in the world (1 John 2:15)? _____

3. Psalm 133:1 tells us, "How good and how pleasant it is for _____

_____ ."

4. Glory should be given to God in the church of Jesus Christ (Eph. 3:21). How does your church bring glory to God? _____

_____

How could it bring even more glory to God? _____

_____

5. Paul promised to pay any debt that one of his new converts might have incurred previously (Philemon 18, 19). How might a similar service be advantageous to a new convert today? _____

_____

6. How do you think a Christian's faithfulness in paying his debts relates to his testimony for Christ? _____

_____

7. According to 2 John 6, what is love? _____

_____

8. Why did the apostle John rejoice (2 John 4)?

_____

9. What is the condition of one who rejects the fundamental truths of Christ (2 John 9)? _____

_____

10. Of what is a person guilty if he supports a false teacher (2 John 10, 11)? _____

_____

"I used to be a Christian." "We don't go to church anymore." "My parents raised me in Sunday School, but I decided that God-business wasn't for me." "My wife taught beginners and I was a deacon, but I guess we just didn't see the need for religion."

Such comments have probably pierced your ears as you witnessed to people about Jesus Christ. John, who served in Ephesus after Timothy, faced the same thing. Looking back over those who had fallen away he said, "They went out from us, but they were not of us: for if they had been of us, they would no doubt have continued with us: but they went out, that they might be made manifest that they were not all of us (1 John 2:19).

Some strayed and some stayed; but one thing was sure—God remained faithful.

Paul's Companions Who Strayed

Demas had been with Paul during Paul's first imprisonment at Rome. But by the time Paul wrote 2 Timothy, Demas had forsaken Paul. He left because he loved this present world (4:10). Perhaps he loved the pleasures, the treasures, the comforts of this world. He no longer considered the eternal reward, as Moses did, but focused his mind on the temporal things.

The Word of God warns each reader about the danger of loving the world: "Love not the world, neither the things that are in the world. If any man love the world, the love of the Father is not in him" (1 John 2:15). No man can serve two masters, and no one can have both the world and God as his loves. Loving the world is so serious because it is evidence that the Father's love is not present in the life.

When Demas forsook Paul, he went to Thessalonica. That city may have been his hometown, for he is mentioned with Aristarchus one place in Scripture, and Aristarchus was from Ephesus. If so, Demas may have packed his bags and gone home, back to his old place, his old job, his old friends and his old ways. What a sad foreshadowing of those today who follow Christ for a while and then return to their old life.

Demas was not the only deserter, unfortunately. No man stood with Paul at his first trial (2 Tim. 4:16). No human being stood as a witness in his behalf, and no one stood as an attorney to represent him. He was alone at that dark and difficult hour. There must have been other Christians in Rome. Some may not have known Paul was there. Others may have forgotten the trial date, for it just was not important to them. And then there were those who held back in fear of what might happen to them if they identified themselves with Paul and Jesus Christ.

As Christ hung dying on the cross, He prayed that the Father would forgive His crucifiers. Stephen made a similar request as the rocks battered him to death. And Paul also asked God to forgive those who deserted him at the time of his need. Do *we* have something to learn about forgiveness?

Paul's Companions Who Stayed

Six people who stayed faithful to Paul gained mention in the closing page of Paul's letter: Crescens, Luke, Tychicus, Erastus, Trophimus and Titus.

Titus is familiar from our study of Paul's earlier letter to him. You will recall that he was in Crete during Paul's time of freedom between the two Roman imprisonments. While Titus was serving there, Paul wrote a letter to him. In that letter Paul asked Titus to meet him at Nicopolis, where the apostle had decided to spend the winter. Probably Titus had joined Paul at Nicopolis after Titus' replacement had arrived in Crete.

Sometime between his meeting Paul and Paul's trial, Titus had departed to Dalmatia (2 Tim. 4:10). There is no reason to believe that Titus had loved the world or deserted Paul. More likely he had left Paul for further ministries in Dalmatia, probably at Paul's direction.

Crescens had gone to Galatia, probably to minister there at Paul's request. Erastus was serving in Corinth. Trophimus had become sick as he traveled with Paul, and Paul had left him at Miletus to recover from his illness.

The only worker in the gospel still with Paul as he wrote was Luke, the doctor (4:11). Luke had joined Paul during Paul's second missionary journey, and he had been with Paul rather consistently ever since. Isn't it interesting that the Gentile doctor Luke would be the only one giving Paul fellowship as he anticipated death?

Tychicus had been sent by Paul to Ephesus, where Timothy was ministering (v. 12). Possibly he was sent to be Timothy's replacement so that Timothy could go to visit Paul. He may have been the courier to take this letter from Paul to Timothy.

Timothy

Timothy was exhorted to be faithful, and he received instructions by which he could demonstrate his faithfulness to the Lord's apostle and so to the Lord Himself.

Paul requested that Timothy leave his post in Ephesus and come to be with Paul in Rome (v. 9). Paul was in a very difficult situation, and he desired the personal companionship of his friend Timothy. All Paul's other fellow workers had either been sent on ministry trips or had deserted.

Paul requested that Timothy come before winter. Travel was dangerous in the winter, and furthermore, Paul needed his heavy coat before the cold invaded the prison.

Paul wanted Timothy to bring his books and parchments (v. 13). The parchments would have been writings made on expensive animal skins, and probably were the Old Testament Scriptures. Even though death loomed close, Paul wanted to study God's Word.

Timothy was to bring John Mark with him when he came to Paul (v. 11). Mark was a beautiful example of restored fellowship. He had been unfaithful, deserting Paul and Barnabas on the first missionary journey. But later things were so completely straightened out that Paul could say of Mark, "He is profitable to me for the ministry."

Faithful Timothy faced a problem in the person of Alexander. Alexander had opposed Paul and done him much evil when Paul served the Lord in Ephesus. Paul suspected that he would continue to oppose the truth of God as Timothy and others proclaimed it. And so Timothy must beware of this enemy of the gospel (vv. 14, 15).

The Lord

Paul's companions in the gospel were a mixed bag. Demas had forsaken him. Everyone had failed to stand with him at his trial. Luke was bravely ministering to him as he wrote. Tychicus was off on a special mission, and probably Crescens and Titus likewise. Timothy himself had been urged to faithfully minister to Paul in very practical ways. So some were faithful, and others were not. And you and I must ask ourselves if we are being faithful as God would desire.

But let's turn from Paul's companions to notice the One with Whom he worked most closely in the cause of the gospel. As Paul neared the conclusion of his letter with its focus on faithfulness, he had no more fitting ending than to turn attention to the faithful One, God Himself. Paul proclaimed the faithfulness of God Who alone was faithful to Paul in his greatest hour of need (4:17, 18).

When Paul had his trial, God stood with him. No human being did, but God was faithful to His promise never to leave. Paul had faithfully carried out the great commission, and Jesus never left him. Paul sensed the presence of God as he endured the agony of his trial.

God strengthened Paul as he stood before the

Roman tribunal. He strengthened Paul so that the preaching might be fully known to the Gentiles. Paul's trial would have been a sensational hearing. Roman governmental dignitaries, beyond the required legal officials, may have packed inside the courtroom. Paul had no lawyer, and so he spoke in his own behalf. Since he was on trial for preaching the gospel, his defense must have included a clear presentation of that gospel.

This situation could easily have been viewed as an "out of season" time for preaching (4:2). Paul could have tried to get himself off the hook. But he saw the situation as a choice time to preach Christ, and God strengthened him to do so.

God delivered His apostle out of the lion's mouth (v. 17). Paul could not have been referring to the lions of the amphitheater, for as a Roman citizen he would not have been subjected to such treatment. "The lion" may have meant Caesar, king of the empire. It may have meant Satan. Paul may have intended the term to convey death, as it does in Psalm 22:21. All three meanings combine nicely, for Satan was the unseen force working through Caesar to bring Paul to death. But God delivered him at that point.

God would deliver Paul from every evil work (v. 18). Paul was going to die soon, so he did not mean that God would keep him from death. Furthermore, God's preservation would extend through death and unto the heavenly kingdom. God would keep Paul from recanting and becoming unfaithful, even though execution loomed ahead. And God would keep Paul safe from the forces of evil who wanted to snatch him out of God's hands and thwart God's plan for his life. If God should allow Paul to be killed, it

Notes

would only be because His plans for Paul had been fulfilled and Paul's work would be done.

And so Paul gave great praise to God. God was faithful to Paul, and Paul would be faithful to God all the way to Heaven, for God was able to keep that which Paul had committed to Him (Paul himself) until that day (1:12).

The closing words of 2 Timothy are a prayer: "Grace be with you. Amen." The word "you" in the Greek is definitely plural, indicating that Paul intended there be other readers of the letter than merely Timothy himself. This letter was addressed to Timothy primarily but not exclusively. It was addressed to the church at Ephesus, as well, and to churches and believers throughout the ages, including you and me.

"Grace be with you." It has been said that all of Paul's theology could be distilled into one word, "grace." In his very last recorded words Paul prayed that all believers might experience the grace of God. The grace of God will strengthen us so we can be faithful to Him as long as He gives us breath. Will you take hold of that grace?